THE CIVIL WAR HISTORY SERIES

NELSON COUNTY

A PORTRAIT OF THE CIVIL WAR

The Kentucky Legislature created the State Guard in May 1860. This allowed volunteer militia units to be organized in each county. This picture was taken at the first encampment at Louisville, August 1860. In the center wearing the top hat is Governor Beriah Magoffin. The Nelson Greys and Stone Riflemen were the Nelson County Units. Captain John Crepps Wickliffe of Bardstown commanded the Greys, and W. Davis McKay commanded the Riflemen.

JULY 28, 1861: Capt. John C. Wickliffe lost his stables, carriage house, and carriage to a fire set by an "incendiary." It was thought that his southern sympathies may have been the reason for the fire.

AUGUST 6, 1861: The Bardstown Trustees allowed the "Home Guard" to use a room in the Market House for meetings.

SEPTEMBER 16, 1861: In Madison, Arkansas, Bloomfield men of Stone Riflemen, 1st Lt. Davis McKay, 1st Sgt. Green C. Duncan, and Henry Clay McKay were mustered in Co. K of the 8th Reg. Infantry CSA.

THE CIVIL WAR HISTORY SERIES

NELSON COUNTY

A PORTRAIT OF THE CIVIL WAR

DIXIE HIBBS

ARCADIA
PUBLISHING

Published by Arcadia Publishing
Charleston, South Carolina

Printed in the United States of America

Library of Congress Catalog Card Number: Applied for

For all general information contact Arcadia Publishing at:
Telephone 843-853-2070
Fax 843-853-0044
E-Mail sales@arcadiapublishing.com
For customer service and orders:
Toll-Free 1-888-313-2665

Visit us on the Internet at www.arcadiapublishing.com

This Civil War-era rifle was discovered with a cache of guns in the upper floor of St. Joseph College's main building in the 1930s. The Xavierian Brothers, who operated the school at the time, gave studentworker Sam K. Cecil one at his request. Who left them and why is another of Nelson County's Civil War mysteries.

CONTENTS

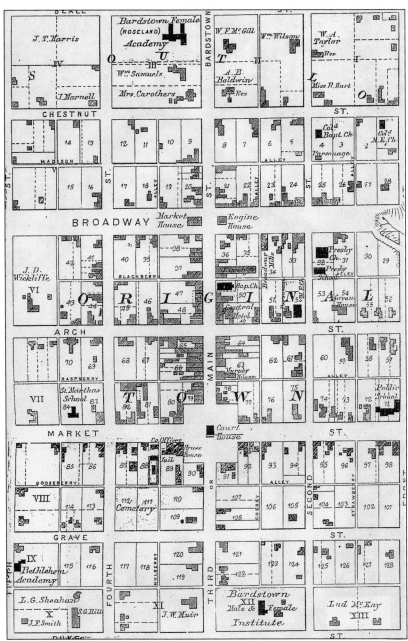

This is an 1882 map of Bardstown. It includes all of the town in 1860, except one block north to the railroad depot and one block west to St. Joseph College and St. Joseph Cathedral. The street names are the same as in the Civil War period, but the east-west street names were changed in the late 1930s to honor famous people in the community. Beall and Broadway remained the same; Chestnut Street became Brashear; Arch Street became Flaget; Market Street became Stephen Foster; Graves Street became John Fitch; and Duke Street became Muir. Most of the buildings represented on this map were there during the 1860s and many still survive today. Bardstown has more than 300 buildings listed on the National Register.

INTRODUCTION

In the Spring of 1861 the war drums were beating throughout the South. Kentucky was holding to a middle line of no involvement. Political maneuvering kept the state government from committing to support for her southern sisters. This stance of neutrality gave the southern sympathizers a sense of security from Union control or invasion of the state. Behind the scenes, the Unionists were plotting to set up recruitment camps, and shipping arms into the state to arm those recruits. The Confederates were also recruiting over the state line in Tennessee. As soon as the union camps opened, they moved up into Bowling Green and accepted soldiers to the cause.

Union camps of instruction were located throughout the state. These camps had a two-fold purpose—first to prepare the new soldiers for military life and battle, and second to occupy the state with troops. This method of intimidation continued for the next four years. The war raged south in Tennessee and Alabama. After the Ohio River was under the control of the Federals, they sought the Cumberland and Tennessee Rivers for access to the heart of the South. The L & N Railroad was only one of the lines necessary to funnel supplies and munitions to the federal armies. Louisville, Kentucky, was the main gateway for supplies, down the river and over the rails. Federal successes in the winter and spring of 1862 encouraged those who believed Kentuckians didn't need to choose sides— "a good Union state but south of the river."

In the summer of 1862, Confederate strategy dictated a show of force: invade the Bluegrass, free those who live under the Federal yoke, and bring the recruitment officers to their doors. The grand plan involved Confederate Kirby Smith going from Knoxville, Tennessee, through southeast Kentucky up to Lexington. Confederate Braxton Bragg came from Chattanooga through Central Kentucky up through Glasgow, Munfordville, Elizabethtown, and then to occupy Louisville. Smith was to join Bragg in Louisville. Unionist Don. C. Buell left Nashville and raced to reach Louisville before the Confederate army, a race which Buell won. He was able to consolidate many new troops into an army which met with Bragg at Perryville. The superiority in numbers of the federals determined the outcome. This was the last time a major move was made to bring Kentucky into the Confederacy. Morgan would make several raids into the state, but his harassment of supply lines and federal troops had more news value than long term effectiveness. Kentucky was an occupied state with martial law, treated like an occupied southern state though in all respects she still remained part of the Union. The actions of some of the Military Commanders and Provost Marshalls would be too much for even those Unionists who helped bring in the rifles and set up the camps. Control of the elections, price control of farm products, corruption, favoritism, imprisonment for minor offenses, and retaliation would soon sour the average citizen toward the Federal Government. This atmosphere of subjection to the military would leave an indelible mark.

Nelson County was in the center of much of the controversy. First, the location of the turnpikes and the railroads dictated the movement of many troops and supplies through the area. Turnpikes were stone-based roads capable of handling wagons and heavy travel in all weathers. Quartermasters were buying grains, livestock, horses, mules, and other army needs along these roads. Shipping these goods south was easy by rail or steamboat to Louisville .

Shorterm soldiers from both sides came back into the state and began to form into bands of marauders. They claimed to be partisan rangers, or the more official Home Guards sanctioned by the military or state, but their actions were those of outlaws. Burning, robbing, and killing were done all in the name of the cause, Union or Confederate. Again Kentuckians chose sides, whichever could or would protect them from the other. This warfare on the homefront continued until the spring of 1865. By this time, many of the returning soldiers were being targeted by the military as guerrillas, and by the guerrillas as fair game. The war was over but Kentucky was still under martial law until September. Returning confederate soldiers were not allowed to wear any part of their uniform or carry guns. Many came back to find their homes burned and their property sold to pay taxes and bills. The Union soldiers did not fare much better in their homecoming. Guerrillas destroyed many public and private buildings. Troops were still stationed around the state, a military presence which started four years before, but it became even more irritating and unnecessary. It is said that "Kentucky didn't secede until after the War," a statement that reflects the attitude of the state in the years immediately following the end of the Civil War.

In 1861 Bardstown was the county seat of Nelson County as it had been since 1785. Other communities in the county were Bloomfield, New Haven, Boston, Fairfield, and Samuel's Depot. Agriculture was the main industry, and historically the county had supplied grains, pork, whiskey, and rope to the southern markets since the 1780s. Nelson County was connected to Louisville by a turnpike and a railroad only one year old. Its private educational institutions were attended by students within and outside the state, particularly from the southern states. Although large plantations in the northeast section were operated with slave labor, the ownership of slaves did not necessarily determine one's support of the Union or for the Secessionists; many families were split in their loyalties. Soldiers from Nelson County fought for both sides during the conflict, but a larger number served the Confederacy than served the Union. The occupation of Bardstown by Union troops began in September of 1861 and ended in September of 1865. As one local woman told later, " I couldn't step out my kitchen door without stepping on a Yankee soldier." Local written histories and family accounts have skipped over this four years of military influence in the county, so that the discovery of thousands of union troops and more than 85 different military regiments passing through the county was quite a surprise. When local historians discussed the Civil War, only Bragg's Occupation in 1862, Morgan's Raids, and the activities of the Guerrillas were reported in detail.

Beginning in April 1861, this book will feature a chronological list of events which affected the county during this time, interspersed with stories, both documented and from folklore, about some of the more notable events. Newspaper accounts are used as a source with the colorful phrases and copy of that period; however, they are only as reliable as the reporters, and rumor was the main reporter. Some correspondents related detailed information, but often the misinformation of the first account is not corrected in follow-up issues. Many accounts written by the soldiers and students of Civil War history have been used for information. *The War of the Rebellion Official Records of the Union and Confederate Armies* was used extensively for military actions and reports. Other official documents are used, but the entire story is not here. Pictures of military people and sites in Nelson County are as rare as hen's teeth. Many people had images of soldiers who went away to fight elsewhere, but few of the events here were captured on film. Drawings and photographs of the soldiers and other camps are used to supplement the story. The intent is to stimulate interest in what happened in one county in Kentucky in a war we neither started nor finished, though the effects are still felt 140 years later.

One

INVASION BY THE NORTH

HOME OF HON. BEN JOHNSON - BARDSTOWN, KY.
ON THE LAWN OF THIS HOME IN 1861 WAS RAISED
THE FIRST CONFEDERATE FLAG - 5000 PEOPLE ATTENDED
CLINE PHOTO 3-A-35

APRIL 1861. The Bardstown Tax List of 1860 reflects a population of 169 Black titheables (over the age of 16), 183 children between 6-18, and 181 white titheables (men over 21). The estimated population of Bardstown was 800.

Local tradition states that the William Johnson house in Bardstown was the site of the first official Confederate flag raising in Kentucky. Nancy Crow Johnson was on the committee of southern women who selected the flag design for the Confederate States of America. When she was telegraphed the final decision, she and her maid sewed the design onto a flag which was publicly raised in front of the home before an estimated 5,000 people.

APRIL 15, 1861. The Bardstown Trustees rented space on the public square for one dollar a week to Funk & Goose, who used it for a Daguerrean Car. This car was a portable photography studio, and the final products were encased in gold trimmed frames. Written on the back of the picture is "Corporal Nicholas M. Wayman, 1st Ky. Vol. Cav. FF 16th 12, at Bardstown, August 1861, native of Marion County." He appears to be holding a sword and a canteen, or possibly a powder flask.

MAY 8, 1861. Ex-Governor Charles A. Wickliffe of Nelson County attended a secret meeting of Unionists at the Capitol Hotel in Frankfort. They planned to supply arms secretly to loyal Union forces at key points in Kentucky where there was a danger that the State Guard would take control for the rebels. President Lincoln supplied 5,000 guns on May 18 to be parceled out to loyalists. On January 29th, Wickliffe had been one of six commissioners to a Peace Conference in Washington.

Consignor.	Consignee.	Description of Articles.	Weight.	Rate.	Freight.	Charge
212 Bowman	Jos Johnson	20 Bbls Whiskey		50	10 00	
Lt On 24 Ky	O Department	20 Bxs Guns Bayonets &c				
"	"	1 Bbl No	} Army			
"	"	3 Tent Poles & Lot Tent Pins	}		10 00	

MAY 13, 1861. The railroad shipping book (hereafter RRSB) lists "Capt. (John C.) Wickliffe (ship) to Henry Lyons (steamboat) 1 canon and fixtures, 1 box merchandise to Louisville." Wickliffe was in charge of the Nelson Greys, a company of the Kentucky State Guards. In 1860, the Bardstown Branch of the Louisville & Nashville Railroad opened the track from Bardstown Junction. This is an entry from the shipping book which listed all the outgoing shipments from January 1860 to summer of 1865. A review of the pages tells of the farm products, whiskey, tombstones, and household items shipped to Louisville and other stops. Many of the items were consigned to steamboats for shipping on the river.

JUNE 21, 1861. St. Joseph College Commencement Exercises were moved up two weeks to accommodate the southern students who were eager to return to their homes. This date would mark the last commencement at St. Joseph's by the Jesuits. A boarding school for young men from 10 to 18 years of age, it was opened by Bishop Benedict J. Flaget in 1820 with local priests as teachers. The Jesuits took over in 1848. In the 1860-61 school year, 118 students were registered from Kentucky, 82 from Louisiana, 22 from Mississippi, and 17 from Missouri. Only 14 were from the northern states. The atmosphere was distinctly southern.

MAY 22, 1861. Alfred Pirtle served with the Citizens Guard of Louisville and, in a journal entry, described prewar camp life at Camp Shelby on the Salt River in Bullitt County. "The regular routine of camp life commenced today. We live as follows. Morning gun and reveille at 5. Surgeon's call at 5:45 when every tent is expected to be in order; the company's parade or street, swept clean and everything prepared for inspection of the Surgeon, who makes his rounds at that hour. Breakfast 6:30. Two men, from each mess of six, cook, changing everyday. The cooks also wash dishes, but on those days do not have any work to do around the tents. Company drills at 7:30, lasting until 9:45, when the Adjutant's Call is sounded and the guard detail, from each company, is made. Guard mounting at 10:00. The Guard are on duty 24 hours and but few get any sleep in that time. The men in camp except the cooks and guard have no regular duty between 10 am and 4 pm. The hours are spent reading, writing, card playing, rowing on Salt River which runs by the camp. Battalion drill from 4 to 5:45. Adjutant's call at 5:55 and Dress Parade at 6 pm which winds up the day. Supper comes off at 7:30. From Supper till 9:30 we amuse ourselves as we please. Tattoo beats at 9:30 which is the signal for all to prepare for bed at Taps at 10:00. All light except those in staff officers tents are extinguished and quiet must reign. If men are found making a noise after this hour and an admonition of the officer of the night does not quiet them, he brings a file of men and marches them off to sleep in the guard tent." The photo is of the Kentucky State Guards at camp at Louisville in August 1860.

SEPTEMBER 24, 1861. William Carothers and Tom Porter of Bardstown set out to "go to war" and join the troops at Camp Charity near Bloomfield. From Carothers' diary entries: "Camp Charity near Bloomfield Ky. was a place where recruits for the Confederate Army were rendezvoused to go South with Col. Crepps Wickliffe. Being anxious to join this army and my mother being opposed as she was a Union woman, I was forced to leave home without telling any of my family goodbye. A bright day, with my friend Tom Porter and our guns upon our shoulders, we passed down the street past the Court house and out Market Street. Dr. Harrison McCown (home pictured) called out to us 'Where are you going boys?' 'To the War' we gaily replied and we passed on. The news was reported at once to my mother and she was advised as I was but seventeen, to get out a warrant and have me arrested and brought home by legal authority. We were out three miles on the Bloomfield road when we were overtaken by the Sheriff Arch Thomas. The sheriff conducted me in triumph to my mother who affectionately told me that if I would wait until I was a few years older then it would be alright with her. My friend Tom went on and went out with his comrades on the march to Bowling Green. A stray shot killed him before he arrived in Bowling Green."

SEPTEMBER 1861. A Bardstown merchant had a lively business in firearms and accessories. The tension of the coming conflict is reflected in these arms purchases from ledger entries of September 1861: "W. W. Metcalfe Navy Pistols at $30.00 each; Arch Wilson A qt powder, 1# Navy Balls, 1 box WP caps; Alex Sayers 3 # Navy Balls, 1 box WP caps; Henry Nichols 2# powder, 4 # lead, 1 box caps; D. H. Linebaugh caps, lead and powder; John Cissel Powder, lead & caps; Thos. H. Crozier Pistol to son; S.G. Adams 1 pistol; John B. Bowman1 Box WP caps, 1 # Powder, 1 pistol $35.00; Henry Nicholls shot & caps; C. C. Wells Navy pistol, 1 flask; E. B. Smith & Co.1 powder flask; Jas. Culver Powder & Lead."

September 22, 1861. Morgan arrived with his men at Camp Charity, seven miles from Bardstown and three miles from Bloomfield. On Friday evening, September 20, knowing that the State Guard was about to be disarmed by the Federal authorities, John Hunt Morgan, commander of the Lexington Rifles (pictured above in August 1860), had the company's arms loaded on two wagons and started toward Lawrenceburg. Morgan and the rest of the company who wanted to join the Confederacy slipped away after dark, the next day riding toward Lawrenceburg and Bloomfield. They were joined by most of the Nelson Greys at a farm located on the Middle Branch of Simpson's Creek. Who arrived first, the Nelson Greys or the Lexington men is not known, but the site was probably chosen by Capt. John C. Wickliffe. Bloomfield's sympathies laid with the South and they could be counted on for support and recruits. It had been reported that the 10th Indiana Infantry was to move to Bardstown, which was not a safe location for confederates to camp. The creek supplied water for men and horses, and the community supplied food and other items without accepting payment, whence came the name "Camp Charity." Rebel-fed rumors of an attack on the Federal troops at Bardstown kept them on alert in their garrison. When Morgan and his recruits left on September 28th, they were uncontested by the Federals as they made their way to Fort Albert Sidney Johnson at Bowling Green. The Nelson Greys were known as Company B. of the 9th Kentucky Regiment and belonged to the 1st Kentucky Brigade, later known as the Orphan Brigade. Other recruits served with Morgan's cavalry.

Dr. Alfred Hynes was a true Unionist. In his house on the Court Square in Bardstown, he not only treated the sick, he recruited troops for the Federal army. A broadside of the time tells all to come to Dr. Hynes on the Court Square to support the United States and the Constitution. Dr. Hynes had one son serving the North and another serving the South. The house had been occupied by many doctors since it was built in 1788.

SEPTEMBER 25, 1861. The *Cincinnati Gazette* included the following: "A traveler left Nashville Friday on a train which only reached the state line. He stayed overnight in a freight car because of lack of accommodations. The next day he jumped on a train of soldiers going to Bowling Green. He says there is a rebel camp of 10,000 men. On Sunday he again joined a train bringing troops and came to within three miles of Munfordsville, where there was a camp of 1200-1400 men. From three miles to Munfordsville he came on foot, then rode to New Haven on the Lebanon Branch of the L & N railroad in an old lumber wagon which he and five others paid thirty six dollars to use. They walked half the distance lest the rotten old vehicle should break down and leave them in the woods. From New Haven to Louisville, arriving on Tuesday, he came by cars, and was informed that that was the last train that would run on the branch road. All of southern Kentucky is occupied by southern troops. The traveler said that about 150 people at Munfordsville were anxious to share with him his seat in the rickety old vehicle to New Haven."

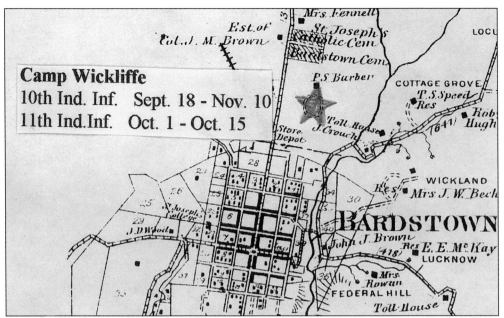

Camp Wickliffe
10th Ind. Inf.   Sept. 18 - Nov. 10
11th Ind.Inf.   Oct. 1 - Oct. 15

SEPTEMBER 18, 1861. The 10th Ind. Infantry under Col. M. D. Manson camped in Bardstown. When they came to Bardstown toward the end of September, their camp was described as being on the high ground between Wickland and the Louisville Pike. It was called Camp Wickliffe in honor of the ex-Governor Charles A. Wickliffe.

OCTOBER 1, 1861. *The Louisville Daily Post* published "Exciting rumors" from Nelson County. "A detachment of five hundred men from the Tenth Indiana Regiment left Louisville and proceeded at once to Bardstown, occupying the place. It is understood that a party of six hundred rebels were entrenched on the farm of Arch Wilson, about half way between Bardstown and Bloomfield, and it was rumored last evening that an engagement had taken place between the Indianas and the rebels with what result, we were not informed."

SEPTEMBER 30, 1861. *The Louisville Daily Post* included the following: "Joseph G. Wilson has just returned from Camp Anderson, Lebanon Jct. [pictured above]. He has been authorized to raise a company of troops to serve three years and hopes to raise his company in the County of Nelson, where he spent his early life. He will immediately open a recruiting office in Bardstown." The 2nd Kentucky Vol. Cav. USA was mustered in at Muldrough's Hill on September 9, 1861. Capt. John D. Wickliffe and Capt. Elijah S. Watts of Bardstown were listed in Company A. They marched with General Rousseau in defense of Louisville in September 1861, and would later return to their hometown with Gen. Don C. Buell's Army in October 1862.

OCTOBER 5, 1861. The 32nd Indiana Infantry Regiment, known as the 1st German Regiment and commanded by Col. A. Willich, marched to New Haven and remained in camp a short time. The October 16 issue of the *Louisville Journal* reported two Union officers, Col. John M. Harlan and Capt. Joseph G. Wilson, were challenged by pickets from Colonel Willich's Indiana regiment about three miles south from New Haven on the Hodgensville road. Ordered to dismount, they tried in vain to prove their identity with passes and letters. They were marched three miles on foot to Colonel Willich's New Haven headquarters. He was also reluctant to accept their statements of loyalty. They were finally identified by some loyal citizens of New Haven, were released, and spent the night in Col. Willich's tent "drowning their sorrows in a basket of Col. Willich's Rhennish wine." This camp picture was drawn by Henry Mosler of *Harpers Weekly* when they had moved further south on the Green River.

OCTOBER 10, 1861. A notice to all tavern and restaurant keepers stated "the law passed by the Legislature is now in force making it unlawful for anyone to sell [liquor] to any officer or soldier, within five miles of any military camp. Fines from $10-100 will be imposed." Of course, this did not prevent the purchase of liquor by the medical department of the army. This barrel says "TOO FOND OF WHISKEY, FORGED AN ORDER ON THE SURGEON."

OCTOBER 12, 1861. The 10th Indiana camped at Bardstown and went to Fredericksburg to investigate the rumor of a rebel cavalry force. They missed the rebels but shot Jacob Grier, a wealthy and prominent Unionist, who threatened them with a shotgun.

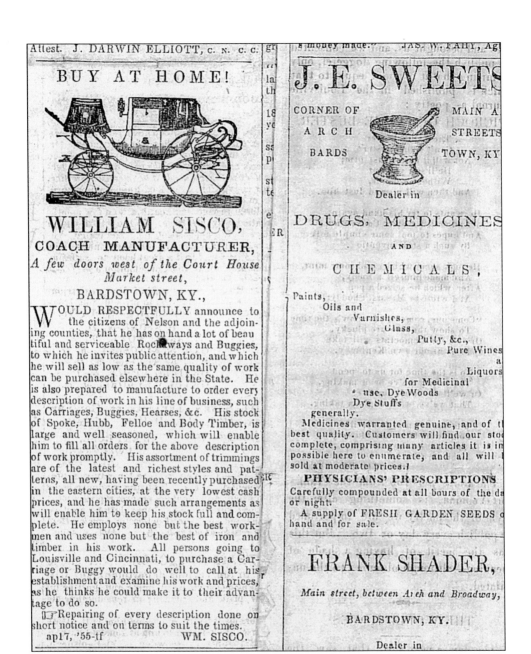

OCTOBER 11, 1861. The RRSB lists "Col. [M.D.] Manson ships one car arms to Louisville."

OCTOBER 12, 1861. The 11th Michigan Infantry, 1200 men, commanded by Col. William J. May, marched into Bardstown to a Camp of Instruction.

OCTOBER 18, 1861. The 11th Ind. Inf. USA left Bardstown after camping there for two weeks.

OCTOBER 22, 1861. The 10th Indiana published a newspaper in Bardstown for "their own amusement" named *The Bardstown Chronicle*. Included with other news was an invitation to attend services held by the regimental chaplain, Rev. Dr. Daugherty, at two o'clock every Sunday in the "grove" at Wickland. Reference to local establishments indicate the Unionist leanings of their owners. These included the Smiley House by E. S. Watts on Main Street, and ads for the Sisco Coach Factory, Hines House, James Hite's Dry Goods store, John E. Sweets & Co. Drugstore, and attorneys Elliott and McKay.

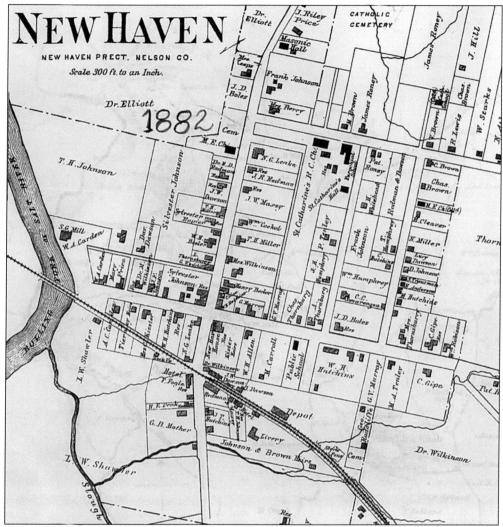

NEW HAVEN

NEW HAVEN PRECT. NELSON CO.

Scale 300 ft. to an Inch.

Dr. Elliott

1882

NOVEMBER 1, 1861. The 16th Ky. USA was camped at Camp James B. Temple at New Haven.

NOVEMBER 10, 1861. The 10th Ind. Inf. left Bardstown for Lebanon.

NOVEMBER 12, 1861. The RRSB listed "Lt. Wilstack Lt. D. N. Sheel, of the 10th Ind. Vol., 9 boxes of mdse. 74 bbl bread, 2 cask shoulders, 1 cask sides, 2 Lbs. Hams, 3 bbls rice, 4 bbls Hominy, 1 bbl sugar, 7 bags coffee, 1 bbl vinegar, 1 bbl salt, 6 boxes soap" (shipped to New Haven).

NOVEMBER 15, 1861. The 34th Ind., with Col. Asbury Steele, was ordered to New Haven, moved to Camp Wickliffe on December 14th, then moved on February 7, 1862. An enlisted man in the 15th Ky. Col. Pope's regiment wrote on December 3 from Camp Pope, New Haven, "our regiment is the healthiest one at this or any neighboring post. This result is due to the excellent sanitary arrangements made by our surgeons. The camp is located on high ground, and receives the full benefit of the cold northwest wind which, after climbing Muldrow's steep breast, rolls on, and passing over the quiet village nestled in the valley, falls ruthlessly upon our defenseless camp, making the men shiver and the tent ropes rattle."

DECEMBER 14, 1861. The 15th Ky. volunteers USA mustered in at Camp Ham Pope near New Haven under Col. Curran Pope on December 14th (Companies A-K listed). Pictured above is an 1882 map of New Haven.

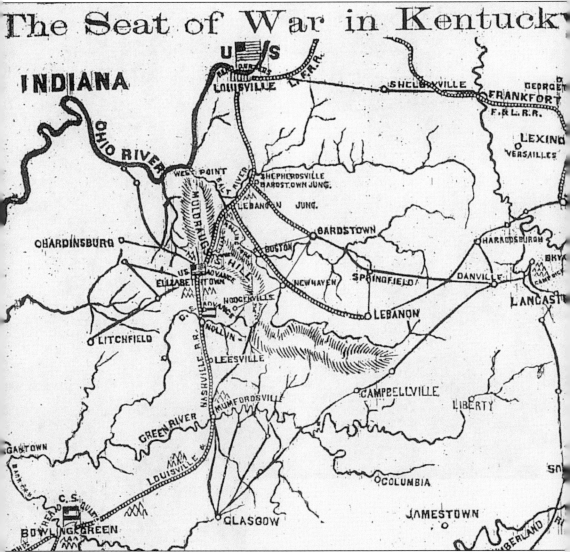

The Seat of War in Kentucky

NOVEMBER 17, 1861. A letter from Gen. Don Carlos Buell to Maj. Gen. Geo. B. McClellan proposed to "form a camp of instruction at Bardstown, which is a convenient place in many respects." This map, originally printed in *The Louisville Daily Journal* in October 1861, shows the location of the troops of the Confederates under Buckner, headquartered at Bowling Green, and the Union headquarters at Louisville and at Elizabethtown. The Federals had camps at Muldraugh's Hill, Shepherdsville, New Haven, Lebanon, and Bardstown. A letter written November 27, from General Buell to Maj. Gen. George B. McClellan, commanding US Army notes "Louisville affords the best base that be taken for land operations from the north upon any part of Tennessee. The railroad to Lebanon curves around to the northeast behind Salt River, giving, besides the Nashville Railroad, three good pike roads, which converge to a point of easy communication for three columns about Glasgowone by the mouth of Salt river, coming into the railroad at Elizabethtown; one by Bardstown and New Haven, and coming into the direct pike road to Gallatin and Nashville; and one by Lebanon, Shepherdsville, and Greensburg into same road; while Lebanon Junction, New Haven, and Lebanon form convenient points for the final departure of as many columns."

December 1, 1861. The 47th Ind. Col. was assigned to Gen. Wood's Brigade. With James R. Slack commanding, they reached Bardstown on the 21st, then moved to Camp Wickliffe (Larue Co.), arriving on December 31st. Pictured is the State Guard Camp at Louisville, August 1860.

December 11, 1861. The 45th Ind. Cos. G, H, I, & K went into camp at Camp Wickliffe (Larue Co.) in December and remained until Feb. 16, 1862.

December 13, 1861. The 49th Ind. Inf. under Col. John W. Ray marched into Bardstown where it went into camp until the 12th of January. The 35th Ind. with Col. John C. Walker commanding left for Bardstown to remain in a Camp of Instruction for six weeks.

December 19, 1861. The 6th Ohio Vol. Inf. marched 60 miles from Louisville to Camp Wickliffe and went into a camp of instruction for the winter. They drilled daily until February 14 when the camp was broken up and they marched to West Point, Ky.

December 21, 1861. James T. Embree of the 58th Ind. under Col. Henry M. Carr, wrote letters from Bardstown.

December 25, 1861. The 50th Ind. arrived at Bardstown where they remained until about the 1st of March.

December 26, 1861. John Ealy of Co. C. 49th Ind. USA wrote that he was at Camp Dumont, at Bardstown, with 2700 troops within 10 miles.

DECEMBER 24, 1861. St. Joseph's College was rented by the Union authorities as a hospital for the sick soldiers of the camps of instruction. When the Federal Authorities rented the college buildings for use as a hospital in December 1861, no one knew that it would be fifteen months before this need was over. They moved in on December 25th with nurses, attendants, and sick soldiers, soon numbering three to four hundred. Besides the army nurses, twelve local women were also attending the sick. In the evening, all returned to their homes, except for three. All day long, large groups of convalescent soldiers and friends strolled along the hallways. Outside, the traffic of wagon trains bringing supplies or sick soldiers was a constant rumble. The Jesuits of the College performed their ministry and noted that "of the soldiers, as many as one hundred and eighty were baptized, a large number of them dying from wounds or disease."

Judge John E. Newman's law office is shown as it looks today. Newman was the leading Unionist in town.

DECEMBER 31, 1861. A soldier of the 77th Ind. USA wrote from Bardstown during the last month. The 57th Ind. USA marched from Louisville to Bardstown. On February 12, they marched on to Lebanon.

JANUARY 1, 1862. St. Joseph College bakery was called into requisition for the baking of bread, not just for the sick soldiers, but for all the troops in the area. Rent for hospital and bakery was $191 a month.

JANUARY 2, 1862. Fr. Charles Truyens left St. Joseph College to become a Chaplain of the 12th Ky. Inf. USA. He developed an illness which caused him to return to the college in the middle of March.

Shewmaker's Livery Stable, shown in this 1880s picture, was typical of the businesses in Bardstown that were concerned about damages from the military buildup in Nelson County.

OCTOBER 17, 1861. A letter to the editor of the *Louisville Daily Journal* expresses the worry about the published accounts of "two thousand Indian warriors, well armed who are no doubt intended to make a dreadful attack" on Louisville. These Native Americans were reported to be with Buckner at Bowling Green and Munfordsville.

DECEMBER 28, 1861. The *Louisville Journal* reported that "General Dumont of Indiana issued a proclamation upon assuming the command of the troops at Bardstown. The people among whom they have come as friends must be protected against all trespasses, excesses, and outrages. With a view to carry these out, he forbids the men to use fences, outhouses, or building materials for fuel, and instructs the officers to permit no rails, boards, or fencing to be used for firewood. He seems determined to preserve every loyal man's home inviolate, and prohibit soldiers from entering any building, public or private, except when granted a permit by their superior officer to attend divine service. Gen. Dumont, regarding 'order as heaven's first law,' allows no one to leave camp without written authority, most strictly interdicts the gift or sale of drinks to the soldiers, and will not permit sutlers to keep intoxicating liquors. No building is to be occupied, unless the necessity is apparent to the Commanding General, and then compensation will be made to loyal owners."

This is a 1912 picture of the Landing Run bridge six miles south of Bardstown on New Haven Pike. All the regiments marching from Bardstown to New Haven and points south crossed this creek.

DECEMBER 26, 1861. The 64th Ohio Vol. Inf. USA arrived in Bardstown. After a short stay they left for Danville, where they engaged in building corduroy roads for the movement of Union supplies to Somerset.

DECEMBER 27, 1861. The RRSB listed "Genl Dumont to self 1 lot Baggage and 4 horses. Shipped to Bacon Creek."

DECEMBER 30, 1861. The 40th Indiana USA went into a Camp of Instruction in Bardstown until February when they left for Nashville.

DECEMBER 31, 1861. The 28th Ky. Reg. Inf. at Camp John B. Temple near New Haven was named in honor of the chairman of the Military Board. Elections were held on January 3, and Lt. Col. Boone and Maj. Absalom Y. Johnson were elected officers. They left camp in February of 1862.

JANUARY 7, 1862. Colonel Whitaker's Kentucky has removed from Bardstown to New Haven.

JANUARY 18, 1862. In New Haven, Martin Baily of the 28th Ky was murdered by a man named Fogle, while on duty at the railroad depot. Fogle turned himself in and claimed self defense.

JANUARY 19, 1862. The Second Indiana Cavalry passed through New Haven en route southward.

William Haines Lytle, a brilliant young officer from Cincinnati, organized the 10th Ohio Regiment and was wounded early in the campaign in western Virginia. He was a cousin of the Rowan family in Bardstown, as John Rowan Sr.'s wife was Ann Lytle. He was a professional soldier, but more famous as the author of a well-known poem of the time, "Antony and Cleopatra," or "I Am Dying Egypt, Dying." After his coming to take command, many referred to Camp Wickliffe as Camp Lytle. Even at Camp Wickliffe, Colonel Lytle found time to write a poem.

IN CAMP

I gazed forth from my wintry tent
Upon the stargemmed firmament;
I heard the faroff sentry's tramp
Around our mountain girdled camp
And saw the ghostly tents uprise
Like spectres neath the jeweled skies,
And thus upon the snowclad scene,
So pure and spotless and serene,
Where locked in sleep ten thousand lay
Awaiting morn's returning ray
I gazed, till to the sun the drums
Rolled at the dawn, ~He comes, he comes.~
1862. Bardstown, Kentucky.

JANUARY 6, 1862. The 4th Ky. Vol. Cav. USA marched from Louisville and went into a camp of Instruction established by Gen. Lytle. (This camp is also known as Camp Lytle, or Camp Morton) They left for Nashville on April 8, 1862.

JANUARY 12, 1862. According to the *Louisville Journal,* "The First and Second Kentucky Regiments are ordered to march without delay and report to Gen. Wood at Bardstown. They will strike tents today and cross from Jeffersonville where they are encamped."

JANUARY 15, 1862. Mother Frances Gardiner of Nazareth wrote to a friend. "I hear there are a great many sick soldiers in town 300 at the college, 100 in the factory near the sisters, they have the smallpox." The cotton spinning factory was located on South Fourth Street. In the summer of 1867, five soldiers would be moved from graves near the factory and taken to the Lebanon National cemetery.

JANUARY 23, 1862. The RRSB listed "Hospital to Surgeon 46th Ind. 1 medical chest, 1 cot to New Haven." The Methodist Church of New Haven was utilized as a hospital during the time of the camps and later skirmishes. It is the building in the background of the picture, and has since burned.

JANUARY 17, 1862. The RRSB listed "QMaster 65th Ohio Vol. to QrMaster 65th Ohio Vol., 1 anvil, 1 forge, 1 box H. nails, 1 vice, 1 box tools, keg shoes, 1 box stores. to Lebanon" and "Owner to E. Gaskin's 51st Ind. Vol., 1 box Testaments, free to Lebanon."

JANUARY 18, 1862. The RRSB listed "QM 57th Ind. Vol. to O. Dept, 9 boxes guns to Louisville."

JANUARY 19, 1862. A telegraph line is expected to be finished in three days along the Bardstown Branch Railroad.

JANUARY 20, 1862. The RRSB listed "Metcalfe to QrMaster 58th Ind., 7 boxes guns to Lebanon and Metcalfe to QrMaster 65th Ohio Vol. 20 boxes Druggs, 1 Med. chest. to Lebanon."

JANUARY 17, 1862. Bishop Martin J. Spalding wrote in his diary "I wrote in Dec'r to Gen'l Wood, commanding at Bardstown, who answered politely, wrote to Mother Superior [of Nazareth] and called himself at Nazareth to assure the Sisters of his protection. He behaved well and like a Ky. gentleman."

JANUARY 19, 1862. The 24th Ky. USA came to Camp Morton where they were assigned to Gen. Thomas Wood's (pictured) division. They left on March 7 to go to Lebanon. Absolom. A. Harrison, of Hardin County at Camp Morton, Boyles Reg. 4th Ky. Cal. USA, wrote "Our camp is four miles from Bardstown on the turnpike leading to New Haven. It was very nice in a woods pasture place when we first came here, but it is knee deep in mud now. I would like to be home but I got myself in this scrape and I will have to stand it. But if I live to get out of this, I will never be caught soldiering again that is certain. We don't get more than half enough to eat and our horses are not half fed and everything goes wrong."

January 21, 1862. This picture is of the 2nd Ky. Regiment in an 1860 camp. The 1st and 2nd Ky. Regiments USA were encamped at Camp Morton near Bardstown. The 1st Kentucky Cavalry Regiment, when it came to Camp Wickliffe that winter, had already been campaigning in Eastern Kentucky. On arriving at Bardstown they found Gen. W. H. Lytle in command. The regiment was ordered to camp on filthy grounds which had just been occupied by the infantry of the army of Ohio.

"In this camp we were also introduced to that species of the genus of parasitic insect, popular known among soldiers by the name of the "grayback," which were destined to adhere to us with the most unyielding tenacity throughout the war, and then were loath to leave us when peace was proclaimed. They made their presence known on the march, around the campfire, and more especially when we folded our weary limbs for sleep or repose. They would feast and have their frolics on the Commanding General's body the same as the humblest Private. The only abhorrence they showed against anything was cleanliness. Everyone could have partial immunity from them by frequent changes of clothing."

" They soon caused us to lose our popularity around the firesides of many of the loyal citizens. The fastidious females seemed to have had a perfect horror of them. Whenever they became so numerous that we would be in danger by being eaten up by them, we could have a short respite by scalding them to death in our camp kittles; or in the cold weather we could hang our clothes on top of our tents and freeze them in one night."

"The Post Surgeon issued strict orders for the men to strip and bathe once a week. The most of us went to a retired woodland, built large fires, heated water and performed our ablutions by the fire. Richard Peach, however, a brave young soldier of Company A, stripped off his clothes and plunged into a creek, was taken with brain fever and only lived a few days."

JANUARY 23, 1862. The big federal encampment south of Bardstown was on the land owned by William Sutherland, a wealthy farmer and distiller. On January 21, two soldiers, Samuel H. Calhoun and Robert Beswick, both of the second Kentucky Regiment, killed a shoat belonging to Sutherland. Sutherland saw them and complained to the camp authorities, even though Calhoun threatened his life if he did so. The two men were given a minor punishment, if any. On the morning of January 23, Calhoun went to Sutherland's house (pictured), found him at breakfast, and told him that one of his soldiers had killed one of his heifers and that he would show him where it was, in a thicket. Sutherland finished his breakfast and went unsuspectingly with Calhoun who shot and killed him. There were tracks in the field from the place where Sutherland's body was found leading toward the camp. Charles W. Thomas, neighbor and friend to the Sutherlands, noticed and followed the tracks across a muddy wheat field. The principal investigator of the crime was Capt. J. H. Green of the 35th Indiana. Suspicion fell on Calhoun and Beswick because of the incident with the pig.

Calhoun had made arrangements for someone else to answer for him at assembly, and disguised himself before going to Sutherland's house so that it was not easy for those who had seen him to be sure in identifying him. His appearance and manner convinced many of his innocence, including the Chaplain, but he told Beswick that he had killed Sutherland. While confined in the Nelson County jail declaring his innocence, he wrote an incriminating note to a comrade which was intercepted. The jail cell and ring to which his leg shackles were attached is pictured.

JANUARY 28, 1862. A court martial was convened on which there were three Colonels, four Lieutenant Colonels, three Majors, and two Captains, one of whom was Captain Green. There does not seem to be any record to that effect, but it could be assumed that the court martial met in the courthouse.

JANUARY 29, 1862. The court cleared Beswick and convicted Calhoun of murder. Shortly after the conviction and death sentence, Calhoun requested permission from Col. William H. Lytle, the commandant of Camp Wickliffe, for Capt. J. H. Green to write a story of his life. Colonel Lytle was quick to give his consent. For the next few days, Green and Calhoun spent all their waking hours together, Calhoun describing his life and Captain Green writing it all down.

FEBRUARY 5, 1862. Approximately 8,000 men, including eight regiments of infantry and two of cavalry on the parade ground of the 22nd Brigade commanded by Col. S. D. Bruce, watched Calhoun hang at 2:00 p.m. The event was described in a letter by Bernard Reilly, Co. F. 7th Penn. Cavalry, dated February 6 and published in the *Pottsville Miners Journal* on February 15 "Yesterday we were ordered to march. At Bardstown, we joined the 35th Indiana, and a Michigan Regiment. The prisoner was brought out, and placed on his coffin, in a wagon. He did not seem to mind it. He laughed and talked as if he was not at all concerned in the affair. We marched 6 miles to Camp Morton, where the scaffold was erected, and from 10-15 thousand volunteers placed around. We being the escort, took up our position very near the scaffold. The prisoner mounted the scaffold, and viewed the large assembly with complacency. He made a short speech, and turning to where his regiment [2nd Kentucky] was, he said in a loud and firm voice, 'Farewell Boys,' at the same time waving his hat and smiling at them. He turned and examined the rope, trying whether the noose would slip right. He then asked for the cap which he leisurely placed over his head and then held his hands behind his back, to be tied. He then stepped on the drop, which fell immediately. He died very hard, kicking for about 2 minutes. I never saw such coolness. The procession was led by the 35th Indiana, then the 11th Michigan, 24th Kentucky, 1st and 2nd Kentucky, 7th Pennsylvania cavalry and the 4th Kentucky Cavalry."

This 1860 photograph shows the Kentucky Home Guard lined up as the soldiers would have been at the 1862 hanging described here.

JANUARY 29, 1862. The 7th PA Cavalry marched two miles beyond the town, encamped in woods on the land of W. R. Grigsby on Springfield Pike. The camp was named after General Thomas who was victorious at Mill Spring. The RRSB listed "Lochel Cavalry to Lochel Cavalry, 7 camp desks, 1 trunk, 4 boxes sundries to Munfordsville."

FEBRUARY 1, 1862. A letter from a 7th PA Cavalryman notes "a number of soldiers stationed through the town as sentinels to guard the Hospitals, Depot, and other public buildings. It is stated that from one to seven soldiers are buried daily, who have either been wounded or sick in the Hospitals of Bardstown."

Pictured is the beginning of the Springfield Pike down the hill from First Street in Bardstown. All eastbound traffic used this road.

FEBRUARY 15, 1862. The *Pottsville Miners Journal* reported "Our Regimental Quartermaster, Thomas H. Rickert you all know him with his assistant John B. Reed of St. Clair, are kept very busy to keep up supplies, both for horses and men, as so many consume a vast amount of feed and provisions some 1100 men, 1206 public, and a number of private animals, which consume daily over 14,000 lbs. of oats or corn, and 18,000 lbs. of hay. This of course, takes a little foraging. Our friends, the sutlers, B. F. Miller and J. L. Shoener, are doing a thriving business and the only difficulty they experience is not being able to keep up the supplies." This *Harpers Weekly* engraving shows the butchering of beef for the Federal Army.

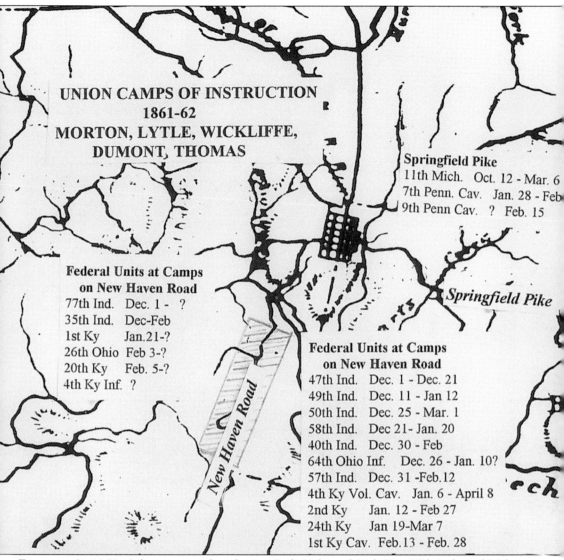

UNION CAMPS OF INSTRUCTION
1861-62
MORTON, LYTLE, WICKLIFFE,
DUMONT, THOMAS

Springfield Pike
11th Mich.   Oct. 12 - Mar. 6
7th Penn. Cav.   Jan. 28 - Feb
9th Penn Cav.   ?   Feb. 15

Federal Units at Camps
on New Haven Road
77th Ind.   Dec. 1 -   ?
35th Ind.   Dec-Feb
1st Ky   Jan.21-?
26th Ohio Feb 3-?
20th Ky   Feb. 5-?
4th Ky Inf. ?

New Haven Road

Springfield Pike

Federal Units at Camps
on New Haven Road
47th Ind.   Dec. 1 - Dec. 21
49th Ind.   Dec. 11 - Jan 12
50th Ind.   Dec. 25 - Mar. 1
58th Ind.   Dec 21- Jan. 20
40th Ind.   Dec. 30 - Feb
64th Ohio Inf.   Dec. 26 - Jan. 10?
57th Ind.   Dec. 31 -Feb.12
4th Ky Vol. Cav.   Jan. 6 - April 8
2nd Ky   Jan. 12 - Feb 27
24th Ky   Jan 19-Mar 7
1st Ky Cav. Feb.13 - Feb. 28

FEBRUARY 3, 1862. A letter states that the 1st, 2nd, 20th, and 24th Ky., 35th Ind., and 26th Ohio were encamped in sight of each other, four miles from town on the New Haven Road. The 4th Ky. was about halfway to town. A letter notes that the 11th Michigan and a PA Cav. under Colonel Williams were about a mile or two along on the Springfield Road. In another letter, F. W. Reed 7th PA at Camp Thomas reported that "today I was helping to finish up a turkey which one of the boys in the company bought. Game is very cheap. Stufed Turkeys that weight 6 or 7 lb for 40 cts. As long as the money last we live good. When that is all we fall back to the old style."

FEBRUARY 5, 1862. The 20th Ky. USA camped five miles from Bardstown and named the site "Camp D. C. Wickliffe" in remembrance of the arduous labors of this gentleman on their behalf before the consolidation under Hanson. Wickliffe was the Secretary of State of Kentucky.

FEBRUARY 8, 1862. The RRSB listed "QrMstr 24th KY to O. Dept, 20 box guns, bayonet, 1 bbl bayonets, 3 tent poles, lot tent pins. to Louisville."

FEBRUARY 13, 1862. The First Ky. Cavalry arrived at Camp Morton, companies K and E noted. They left on February 28th.

33

FEBRUARY 15, 1862. The *Pottsville Miner's Journal* stated "You will of course expect to hear something in regard to secession in this vicinity. We are in the midst of enemy country and the expression of their sentiments is only prevented by the vast number of Union forces stationed at various points in their immediate vicinity. Gen. Buell, however, is watching them and they hate us Lincoln hordes, as they call us, especially the Calvary portion of them, as much as old Nick himself." Gen. Don Carlos Buell is pictured.

FEBRUARY 20, 1862. A letter to McClellan from Buell's chief of staff reported that "Thomas's Division just arriving in Bardstown." General George Thomas was ordered to move Union troops from Somerset, Lebanon, and Danville to Louisville to board transports to Nashville. The rainy weather made quagmires out of the roads, delaying the soldiers.

FEBRUARY 24, 1862. A diary entry of Otis G. Gerould of 7th PA notes "There was 11 regts. passed towards Louisville and 3 Batteries artillery." The entry was written while he was at Camp Thomas.

FEBRUARY 27, 1862. The RRSB listed "Sutlers 2nd Ky. to Sutlers 2nd Ky., 3 chests, 2 boxes to Munfordsville."

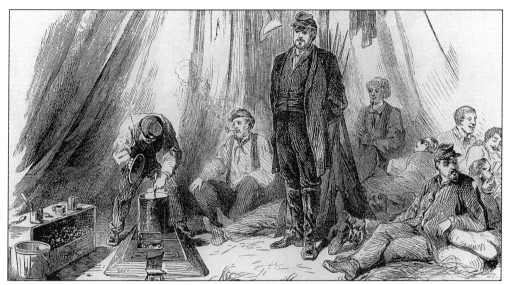

FEBRUARY 17, 1862. Camp Thomas moved to higher ground a "short distance east of the old camp." The horses were to be kept from the streets of the camp to prevent the mud from becoming impassable. A letter of 7th PA Cav. reports that "this is a great country for corn cakes, it being I believe the chief subsistence of the 'dwellers therein' . . . a good hot Kentucky corn cake is the desire and joy of the soldiers." The letter also included a complaint that "These southerners won't take pennies in exchange for goods. Nothing less than 'half dimes' circulate here. If you want an apple, you are obliged to take 10 for five cents, or else take one for the same price."

FEBRUARY 19, 1862. A letter signed by 7th PA Cavalryman Thomas Dornblaser gives details about camp provisions. "We have plenty to eat, but seldom soft bread good when it comes. The health in camp generally, is improving fast. There are regiments encamped all around us, and regiment after regiment passing down the pike."

FEBRUARY 27, 1862. The 7th Reg. PA Cavalry left Camp Thomas, marching 18 miles to Camp Buell, one mile past New Haven, camping "within 200 yards of the place that President Lincoln learned his alphabet." Abraham Lincoln went to school for a three-month term at Zachariah Riney's "Blab school" when his family lived at Knob Creek, about three miles away. It was the only formal schooling he obtained. His teacher, Mr. Riney, is buried at the Abbey of Gethsemane where his grandson was a monk. This is a 1912 photograph of the log school.

MARCH 10, 1862. Joseph Hart of Bardstown was arrested by Col. Jesse Bayles and Capt. John Kurfiss of the 4th Ky. USA for unstated crimes. Hart's family immediately asked Judge Linthicum to issue a writ of Habeas Corpus which was ignored, and he was sent to the prison in Louisville. Hart was a police judge of Bardstown, a saddler by trade, and after the war sued the two officers for damages because of their actions. This pass was required to go through any military lines, ride the train, stay on the streets after 9 o'clock, and indicated one's loyalty to the government. It was printed in Bardstown in 1862.

MARCH 1, 1862. Col. Charles C. McCormick of the 7th PA Cav. wrote in a letter "about a week ago, we were encamped in wood and one morning when I looked out of my Marquee the ground was covered with snow about 3 inches deep. The wood consisted of large poplars, large elms with their drooping limbs, maples & etc. Here and there interspersed with scrub pine from 10 to 20 ft high . . . occasionally you would see a large poplar log, perhaps 80 feet in length, stretched along among the tents [these trees are often more than four feet in diameter] Every tree in the wood seemed like a sheet of snow. Small pines were bent to the ground, and every limb in the woods seemed breaking down with the weight of the snow, which remained on the trees for two days. Only imagine 1100 soldiers, 1160 horses & 130 mules. Our tents smoking at the top around two sides of the camp was a ravine where large rough rocks projected and guide a stream of water ran fiercely down. It was a beautiful sight for those who could appreciate it and such, I know will never forget it."

MARCH 11, 1862. Absolom A. Harrison's company acted as provost guards in Bardstown, living in a vacant lot. Unpleasant duty each day is "burying the soldiers who die in the hospitals. There is about six hundred in the hospitals at this place and they die at the rate of about four per day. We also have to put out patrols of 5 or 6 men to walk around town and arrest every soldier without a pass or drunken men and put them in jail until they can get sober." These buried Union soldiers were removed from their first resting places and moved to the National Cemetery at Lebanon in the summer of 1867.

MARCH 29, 1862. Bardstown Trustees issued an order prohibiting slaves from wearing cast-off soldiers' clothing because of the epidemic of smallpox in the camps of instruction.

MARCH 24, 1862. The RRSB listed "H. Schlesinger to self in Louisville, 6 camp chests, 5 boxes Mdse, 1 can c oil, 2 boxes cheese, 1 keg, 2 Barrel Molasses. 1 bbl bedding, 2 buckets, 3 bundles cots, 1 lamp, 5 bbls mdse, 1 stove, 2 bundle pipe, 1 desk, and 1 chair." There was no charge for shipping which indicates it was government merchandise. This *Harper's Weekly* sketch of the inside of a tent shows many of the items Schlesinger was shipping. He could have been a sutler who operated as a general store for the troops.

APRIL 1, 1862. Enoch Clements of Nelson County was charged with operating a "bawdy house," considered a "common nuisance."

APRIL 5, 1862. Rev. Charles Atkinson was pastor of the Bardstown Methodist Church during the time of the occupation of Bardstown by federal troops. The provost Marshall Captain Jonathan Green issued an order that all the churches should be closed unless the pastors would "pray for the success of our army." Rev. Atkinson was known to be a southern sympathizer, and people were curious to see how he would get over the difficulty. When Sunday came, the church was opened as usual and a large crowd was in attendance, including Captain Green. In the course of his opening prayer, Reverend Atkinson asked a blessing on "our army" and prayed that it might be successful, adding in a lower voice, "Oh Lord, thou knowest which army I mean." This building was constructed after the Bardstown Fire of 1856. The fire started on the southwest corner of Second and Market Streets and raged north along both sides of Second Street. It burned the previous church that was located on lot 58. The gothic windows and steeple were added to the church in the 1890s. On May 24, 1998, a lightning fire caused great damage to the roof and steeple. The church has been repaired as seen in this photo.

JUNE 6, 1862. St. Thomas Church and Seminary was located about three miles south of Bardstown on the New Haven Pike. The Union camps of instruction in the winter of 1862 were one half mile away. Some of the seminarians witnessed the hanging of Samuel Calhoun for the murder of their neighbor, William Sutherland. The chaplain of the 35th Indiana, Father Cooney, visited the seminary and brought the regimental band to entertain. The 35th was composed of Catholics who went to confession and holy communion before leaving the area.

APRIL 30 TO MAY 5, 1862. The RRSB listed "Lt. Keeler to Capt. Symonds [Quartermaster] 75 bbl flour, 100 bbl pork to Louisville. [4 cars] 60 sacks coffee, 40 bbls hominy, 8 bbls beans, 13 bbls rice, 562 boxes H bread, 118 boxes soap, 75 bbls flour to Louisville.", 198 boxes H. Bread, 23 boxes soap, 8 boxes tea to Louisville."

JUNE 2, 1862. "Daguerrean Artist should move his car from the Public Square" appeared in the Bardstown City Minutes.

JUNE 6, 1862. The RRSB listed "Gen. Ward [pictured] to Gen. W. T. Ward, 3 boxes goods and 1 horse to Louisville."

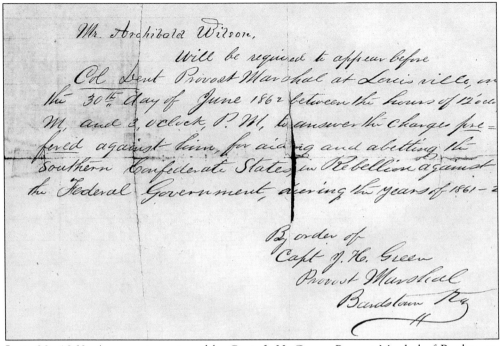

JUNE 28, 1862. A warrant was issued by Capt. J. H. Green, Provost Marshal of Bardstown, for the arrest of Archibald Wilson, plantation owner, for "aiding and abetting the Southern Confederate States." The warrant reads "Mr. Archibald Wilson, Will be required to appear before Col. Dent Provost Marshall at Louisville, on the 30th day of June 1862 between the hours of 12 o'clock and 3 o'clock PM. to answer the charges prefered against him, for aiding and abetting the southern Confederate States, in Rebellion against the Federal Government, during the years of 1861-2 By order of Capt. J. H. Green, Provost Marshall, Bardstown, Ky." The charges may have been based on the reported camping of Morgan's troops on his property in September 1861. This unproven claim was published in the *Louisville Journal*. His son, Isaac Wilson, served with Gen. John H. Morgan.

JUNE 1862. "Hardscrabble" was the name of the plantation which Arch. C. Wilson and his family hurriedly left when he received the warrant for his arrest in June of 1862. He asked his neighbors to watch after the plantation and he fled to Canada. The RRSB indicates that he returned by May of 1863, when he shipped lard and flax seed to a dealer in Louisville. Later shipments included the farm products of wheat, hogsheads of tobacco, and bags of wool.

Two

INVASION BY THE SOUTH

AUGUST 22, 1862. In Kentucky the Loyalty Oath is required of jurors, common school commissioners, teachers, college professors, and Ministers of Gospel, before they can perform marriages. This is an 1859 photograph of the Bardstown Female Institute on South Third Street in Bardstown operated by the Methodist Church. The young man in the middle is Charles T. Atkinson . His mother and father conducted the school. The Rev. Charles Atkinson was a strong Southern supporter and did not take the oath.

JULY 11, 1862. Colonel John H. Morgan was on his first raid to Kentucky when his raiders fought a skirmish at New Hope Station in Nelson County. As he came up from the South, his first objective was Lebanon, which was a sizeable federal supply base garrisoned by about 65 troops under Lt. Col. A. Y. Johnson. In order to keep Lebanon from being reinforced, Morgan sent a detachment under Capt. Jack Allen to block the railroad from Louisville. Just before midnight on July 11, at New Hope Station, Allen's command met a train carrying the 60th Indiana regiment, commanded by Colonel Owen. There was a lively little engagement in the darkness. The rebels were outnumbered and fell back with the loss of one man, a Kentuckian from Owen County said to have been named Forman. The Federal Commander was concerned, however, that the tracks might be torn out behind him, trapping the train, and at about 3 o'clock in the morning he ordered it back to New Haven. He came back at daylight, but the Rebels, except for the one dying cavalry man, had disappeared.

JULY 11, 1861. Morgan did not get to Nelson County on his first raid, but Capt. Jack Allen and his men were reported seen in Bloomfield. The *Louisville Journal* reported on July 26 "The rebels in and around Bloomfield in this state brought corn, oats, and hay into that town for John Morgan & Co., three days before the bandit chief and his gang arrived there. They knew all his plans beforehand and cooperated with him. They should suffer the penalty of their treason." Joshua Gore of Bloomfield was reported as having entertained "atrocious rebels" during their late stay in that place, "Why should not he himself be entertained in a military prison?"

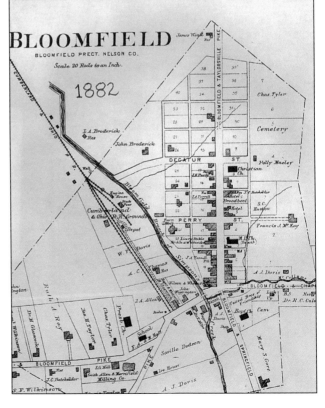

Bragg and the rebels were coming, and Judge John Newman assisted the Federals in evacuating Bardstown. He was widely known as a Unionist, so he may have left his flag flying on his house.

AUGUST 28, 1862. The RRSB listed "Lt. L. J. Keeler to A.G. Hull, 34 boxes Military Mdn. to Louisville."

SEPTEMBER 4, 1862. The RRSB listed "Qr Master Keeler Col. Swords, 1 car QM and Commissary Goods to Louisville."

SEPTEMBER 6, 1862. The RRSB listed "Dr. Newman [William] to Col. Swords, 1 car hospital goods to Louisville." Two hundred convalescent soldiers and government stores arrived in Louisville from the Hospitals in Bardstown.

SEPTEMBER 9, 1862. The *Louisville Journal* reports that "The mailcarrier, who performs the service between this city and Bloomfield, Ky., arrived from Bloomfield Monday evening on horseback, having been compelled to abandon his stagecoach. A party of rebels stole five of his horses a day or two ago, leaving him without sufficient stock to run the coach."

SEPTEMBER 10, 1862. Company G of the 8th Ky. Volunteer Reg. Calvary CSA mustered in at Bardstown. Of 109 members, 105 enrolled in Nelson County. They would later ride with Morgan.

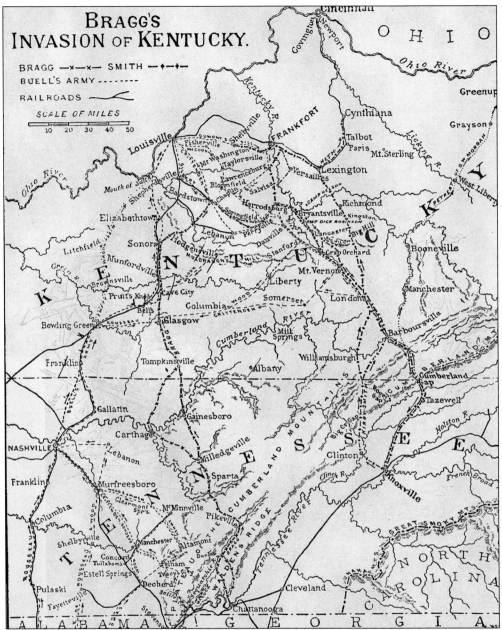

SEPTEMBER 22, 1862. Gen. Braxton Bragg's Army of the Mississippi arrived in Bardstown. This map indicates the routes taken by Gen. Bragg and the Army of the Mississippi when he came from Chattanooga, and Major Gen. Kirby Smith when he invaded Kentucky from Knoxville. Smith continued on to Lexington. Bragg went the western route to Munfordsville, then turned east toward Bardstown. Lack of food for the army was the reason to turn eastward instead of continuing toward the Union stronghold of Louisville, which was the original plan. General Don Carlos Buell's Army of the Ohio came from northern Alabama to try to outrun Bragg's army to Louisville. His march paralleled the Confederate army until Bragg turned toward central Kentucky.

SEPTEMBER 1, 1862. "This old country town is yet a stubborn place yet not as much so as it was a few weeks since. Secesh is on the bide, and has been at intervals for a month past. Colonel Hollis's visit checked them some, and a few days since the 68th Indiana Colonel King, made its entrance, the fine martial band playing Yankee Doodle. Sour countenances from all secesh smiles and cheers from all the Union citizens, male and female. It was a glorious time for some, a grating time for others. The regiment encamped near the town and rested the men three days and nights, and then struck and left. On Sunday noon they struck their tents, and in twenty five minutes after they were in a line and in thirty minutes marching out the Springfield Pike. The citizens were taken completely by surprise as they marched steadily forward, led by their commanders. There goes the best regiment that ever passed these streets, says one. The most moral and wellbehaved, says another. No swearing or disorderly conduct says another. As ever yours, A LOYAL MAN." (*Louisville Journal*)

SEPTEMBER 22, 1862. The Confederate Flag flew on top of the courthouse after General Bragg's Army of the Mississippi occupied Bardstown. The *Louisville Journal*, reported on October 6, 1862 that "A man named Crouch, who was formerly employed on the Bardstown junction of the Louisville and Nashville Railroad, is the rebel who took the Federal Flag from the Courthouse in Bardstown and placed the rebel rag there. He now has command of a company in the rebel army." Could this be N. A. Crouch who operated a carriage manufactory in Bardstown from "1857 until the fall of 1861 . . . when he was seized with the War fever then prevalent and determined to quit his business and turn soldier?"

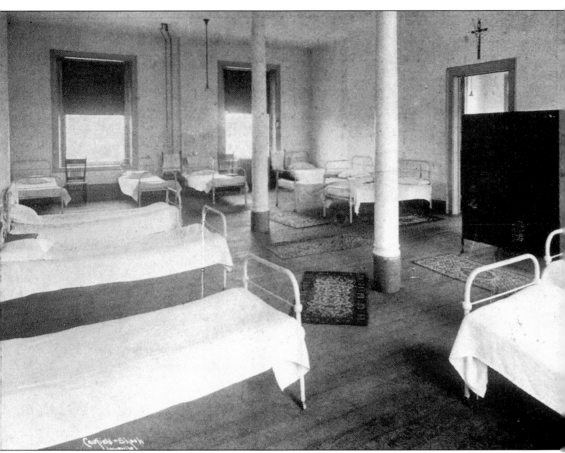

SEPTEMBER 23, 1862. General Bragg asked for the use of the St. Joseph College buildings on the same terms as the Union, with the rent being $175. Father Verdin welcomed numerous former students from the ranks of Confederate troops. He was able to convince them to prepare their souls by confession. Shortly after this time, many of them lost their lives at the Battle of Perryville, among them Gen. Sterling A. Ward of Alabama. This is a 1926 view of the third floor dormitory in the main section of Spalding Hall. Pictured is one quarter of the space on this floor that was used as a ward during the war. The Union army leased the college from December 1861 until March 1863 for use as a hospital. Their training camps, located south and east of Bardstown, had soldiers from Kentucky, Michigan, Illinois, Wisconsin, Minnesota, Ohio, Indiana, and Pennsylvania, all of whom brought their own germs. The college had beds, bedding, and cooking facilities to provide medical care for these sick soldiers. After the Union soldiers left in September 1862, the Confederates brought their injured and ill here until they were displaced in October 1862 by Buell's soldiers. Found in Nelson County on a slip of paper buried in an old book was the following statement "J. H. Mitchel, Co. C 33 Miss Died Sept. 23 1862 Beried on Weatherous creek on the second Branch from the creek and about 200 yards from the Skipers Spring between two wild cherry trees South of the Spring."

September 25, 1862. Sister Marietta Murphy, SCN, then a school girl, writes of her memories of Nazareth during the war. "Before Bragg's Army left the Nelson County Fairgrounds, Generals Bragg, Hood, [this must be Hardee, but the account says Hood] and Buckner paid a visit to the Academy. General Buckner was just released from Camp Chase where he had been prisoner and he looked like one from the grave. Bragg and Hood [Hardee] with their staff officers in Confederate uniform excited great enthusiasm among the southern girls . . . when the gala procession had entered the recreation hall, jubilant voices sang 'Dixie,' 'Jump into the Wagon,' 'The Southern Girl,' and other favorites. General Bragg leaned against a central pillar and listened while the youthful minstrels sang, but the old warrior smiled not. The younger Knights however did smile and chat gaily. General Buckner was the center of attention." Pictured is the Recreation Hall where this affair was held.

SEPTEMBER 24, 1862. Gen. Simon B. Buckner issued a proclamation at Bardstown directed "To The Freeman of Kentucky" calling attention to the fact that the armies of Smith and Bragg were in Kentucky, "come to relieve you of the tyranny with which the North has so long oppressed you."

SEPTEMBER 26, 1862. John Forsythe, a newspaper reporter from Mobile, Alabama, traveling with Bragg's staff wrote the proclamation "To the People of the North West" which Bragg published in his own name in Bardstown on this date. Since no newspapers were printed in Bardstown at this time, one has to wonder if they brought their own press or confiscated one.

SEPTEMBER 27, 1862. Gen. Braxton Bragg addressed the people of Kentucky telling them that this was their last opportunity to volunteer their services in the Confederate Armies, then left for Danville. He was very disappointed with the Kentuckians' response.

This is the Old Star Tavern on the Louisville Pike. It was owned by Joseph Forman and legend has it that it was used as a stagecoach stop. This was the headquarters of Forrest and later Wharton when they were between Buell's army in Louisville and Bragg's in Bardstown, scouting and keeping in touch with the enemy.

SEPTEMBER 24, 1862. Col. John Wharton brought the 8th Texas, "Terry's Texas Rangers," from Boston to Bardstown in this afternoon, He would shortly replace Forrest.

SEPTEMBER 25, 1862. Gen. Nathan Bedford Forrest was relieved to return to Tennessee.

SEPTEMBER 27, 1862. Col. John. A. Wharton reported from High Grove the information from citizens and scouts. He asked to be sent $300 in US or Ky. money to use in secret services.

September 26, 1862. Sylvester Johnson at New Haven entertained Col. Joseph Wheeler and staff as they were guarding the movement of Bragg's Army from Munfordsville through New Haven into Bardstown. Bragg's army, according to Julia Barry Healy, writer of the article published in the *Louisville Times* in 1906, had taken three days to pass through New Haven. Last came the rear guard Cavalry commanded by Colonel Joseph Wheeler. He was invited to breakfast by Mr. and Mrs. Sylvester Johnson at their home in the center of New Haven. Despite the wartime prices and shortages, the Johnsons and their cook, Aunt Mary Price, were determined to have a memorable meal for the occasion. Four of Wheeler's staff officers turned up in fresh uniforms that morning, quite a contrast from the tired and dusty riders of the day before. Even while eating breakfast in the company of seven sympathetic townspeople, the war could not be forgotten. The Federals were at Elizabethtown, only 18 miles away. During the meal, a servant lad bringing in a load of wood for the cook stove dropped it in the woodbox with a crash. Instantly on the alert, Colonel Wheeler electrified the guests with a sharp demand "What's that?" Aunt Mary, serving the meal, reassured them it was just one of her boys in the kitchen. Other guests were Mrs. Henry Beeler, Mrs. John J. Barry, Mrs. J. D. Bowles, Miss Eliza Smith (who married Stephen Clark of Fairfield), Miss Susie Boone, later the wife of Dr. Al Smith of Bardstown, Miss Julia Barry who married Dr. John Healy of Marion County, and Miss Xavier Barry, who married William Hocker of Marion County.

SEPTEMBER 28, 1862. Union troops from the 1st Ky. and 2nd Indiana Calvary captured the 3rd Georgia Cavalry Reg. at New Haven. The story begins when Dr. Wilson of Union sympathies eluded the pickets and rode the 18 miles to Elizabethtown. Meeting with the 1st Kentucky Union Cavalry and 2nd Indiana Cavalry, he gave them full information on the Confederates, including the location of their outposts and pickets. He offered to guide an attack. Colonel Wolford, commanding the 1st Kentucky cavalry, designated 22-year-old Capt. Silas Adams to lead the force to attack the Georgia Confederates. A Lt. Col. Stewart commanded another detachment from the 2nd Indiana Cavalry. They started about 9 p.m., with the intention of reaching the rebel outpost just before dawn. The night was very dark but clear, and there had been a long drought. The road was covered deep in dust, making the tread of the horses almost noiseless. The squad in advance, told by the guide where the first pickets would be, advanced quickly, then made a final dash and summoned the two pickets to surrender, which they did, later saying, "You are so covered with dust and look so gray, we thought you were our own men charging on us to frighten us." Shown here is a *Harpers Weekly* engraving of a troop on the march fording a stream in Kentucky.

At the bottom of the hill they captured the main body of pickets, again without making any noise. The enemy's camp was now in sight, and Captain Adams ordered a charge. "The 1st Kentucky thundered through the wooden bridge across the Rolling Fork, and on through and beyond the surprised and frightened village. The front companies passed by the camp and surrounded it." The conversation that took place when Captain Adams ripped open the Rebel Colonel's tent and ordered him to come out and surrender went as follows. The Colonel was outraged: "Who the hell are you, giving me such peremptory orders?"

"I am commanding the First Kentucky Cavalry."

"But what is your rank?"

"I am a Captain in command of a regiment, But I have no time to quibble about rank."

"But let me have a few minutes to consider."

"Surrender in two seconds, or I will blow your d....d head off."

Pictured is a Kentucky Home Guard's camp in 1860. The Georgia Camp might have looked like this with more tents.

SEPTEMBER 28, 1862. Gen. Leonidas Polk was headquartered first at the Crozier house, then at the Murphy Farm on the Springfield Pike. Polk was in command of the Right Wing of the Army of the Mississippi which was camped on the east side of Bardstown. Judge Felix Murphy lived at Maywood, the home of his wife's family about three miles out the pike. The grounds were flat and fed by good springs—ideal for camps. Gen. Braxton Bragg CSA left Bardstown for Lexington to confer with Gen. Kirby Smith, leaving General Polk in charge. Polk moved into Bragg's former quarters at Edgewood and took command of the whole army. Gen. Benjamin Cheatham was put in command of the Right Wing with his headquarters on Mill Creek.

The Left Wing was commanded by Major General William J. Hardee, whose headquarters at Bardstown were at Joseph Brown's house. The Left Wing Division generals were: Brig. Gen. James Anderson, Brig. Gen. Thomas M. Jones, Maj. Gen. Simon Buckner, Brig. Gen. Sterling Wood, Cavalry Commanders: Col. John Wharton, and Col. Joseph Wheeler. A Brig. General Jackson was assigned the military command of Bardstown itself.

SEPTEMBER 30, 1862. From the headquarters of the Cavalry Brigade at Boston, Col. Joseph Wheeler issued orders concerning surprise attack and mutual aid, "The command must under all circumstances sleep on their arms."

OCTOBER 2, 1862. A report from the Brown home in Bardstown stated "General W. J. Hardee was sending messages at 3 AM and 8 AM to Col. Wheeler trying to obtain information about the Federal advances."

OCTOBER 3, 1862. Many country people and some Confederate cavalry were in Bloomfield. The people had been drawn by the report widely circulated that Dr. David W. Yandell, a long time leading physician of Louisville, and for a year or more a Surgeon General in General Bragg's army, would address the people in the Baptist church on the existing war. By eight o'clock the church was filled and Dr. Yandell delivered his message from the pulpit. The Bloomfield Baptist Church was erected in 1827. It was occupied at different times during the war years by the Federal Troops. On August 9, 1862, the Bloomfield Baptist Church minutes included the following "The church met after preaching adjourned. The Federal Cavalry from Lebanon being here, Some of our members were deterred from the church meeting." The May 5, 1864 Bloomfield minutes read "Sister Kate Thixton Tichenor, who moved to Missouri some 4 years ago, and being driven from home and church there, received by this church without a letter from her church in said state." In 1865 the Elders proposed petitioning the "Government at Washington for remuneration" for the damages done to the building and grounds. No record is found of whether or not they were paid for the damages.

OCTOBER 1, 1862. Pictured here is a 1915 view of Edgewood, the home of Ben Hardin on South Fifth Street in Bardstown. Ben Hardin Helm, the grandson of the builder, was born in this house in 1831. He was the brother-in-law of Abraham Lincoln, and a General in the Confederacy. The home of Judge Thomas Linthicum in 1862, it was the headquarters of Gen. Braxton Bragg and Gen. Leonidas Polk during the Confederate occupation of Bardstown. The Victorian-style porches on the front were added by 1886. In the years after the Hardin family left the home, it served as the residence for the Linthicum, McKay, and Muir families. In the 1940s, Harry Tuer replaced this porch with a two-story, columned porch.

OCTOBER 3, 1862. Polk calls a council of Wing and Divisional commanders to discuss Bragg's order to proceed to Frankfort by way of Bloomfield. This controversial meeting was used in the testimony during the review of the Perryville Campaign. Bragg's orders to Polk were to "move with all available force via Bloomfield to Frankfort to strike the enemy," but when Polk received information that Buell was closing in from Louisville, he called his Division and Wing Commanders who unanimously endorsed his views to move on the route (previously) indicated by Bragg toward Camp Breckinridge. He moved the army toward Danville Harrodsburg by way of Springfield.

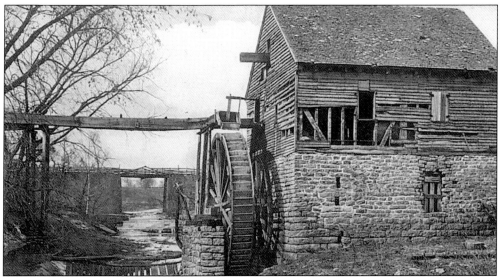

OCTOBER 3, 1862. General Polk and the Army of the Mississippi left Bardstown going toward Springfield. Their baggage train would be strung out for ten miles. Looking upstream from the old millsite is the view of the bridge over Town Creek. Everyone leaving the town going east either to Bloomfield or Springfield must cross this bridge and turn right on the Springfield Pike or left for the Bloomfield pike. The mill was the background for many pictures of the late 19th century. It was torn down in 1901.

Looking east from First Street in Bardstown, this view shows the Springfield Turnpike road as it begins to pass by Federal Hill, the home of the Rowan family. All of the Center Corp of Bragg's army and later Buell's army would pass down the hill, cross a wooden bridge over Town Creek, and continue eastward.

OCTOBER 7, 1862. A report from George G. Garner AAG from Harrodsburg stated "The General commanding [Polk] takes pleasure in bringing to the notice of the army under his command the gallant and brilliant charge made by Col. John A. Wharton, commanding the Cavalry of the Right Wing, against a large force of the enemy near Bardstown, Ky. on the 4th Inst. Being posted four miles on the Louisville Pike, which, as he believed, Col. Wharton occupied and guarded the town of Bardstown and its approaches. Col. Wharton received sudden intelligence that the enemy in force were within half a mile, to the east of the pike between him and Bardstown. Immediately ordering his battery to follow after as soon as possible he put himself at the head of the Texas Rangers and rode at half speed to the point of danger. In thirty minutes he passed the four miles and then found the 1st and 4th Kentucky, 3rd Ohio and 3rd Indiana regiments of Cavalry four times his own number drawn up on the road and behind houses to receive him. In their rear, but not in supporting distance, was a battery of artillery and a heavy force of infantry. The enemy's Cavalry was partially drawn up in columns of eight, prepared for a charge and the rest as a reserve. The enemy was allowed to approach within forty yards, when Col. Wharton ordered a charge. The fearless Rangers responded nobly to the order, and in a few minutes the whole force of the enemy was drawn in confusion from the field with a loss of fifty killed and forty prisoners, among the latter a Major" [Major Watts of Bardstown]. This 1880s photograph depicts the Fairgrounds Building.

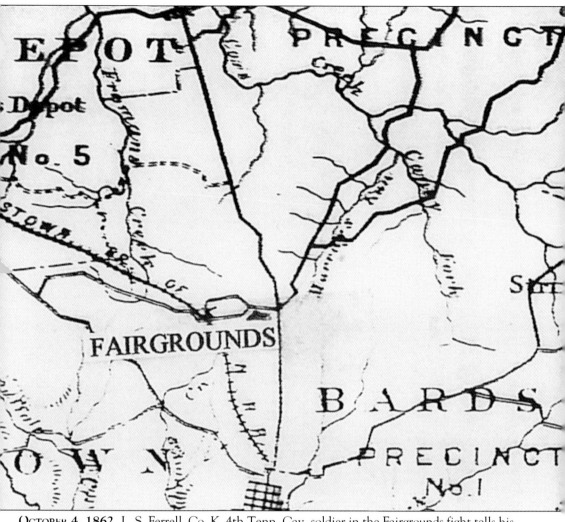

OCTOBER 4, 1862. L. S. Ferrell, Co. K, 4th Tenn. Cav. soldier in the Fairgrounds fight tells his story: "When within a mile or two of Bardstown a rumor reached us that a heavy force of Federal Cavalry had slipped in between us and the town. Of citizens who passed us some said there were no Federals between us and the town and others reported 'a Yankee line of battle across the pike at the fair grounds.' To settle the question, Gen. John Wharton directed Capt. Anderson to take his company and ascertain the facts. We went at a gallop, and soon found them in line and 'ready for business.' Sending a courier hurriedly back to General Wharton, Captain Anderson called at the top of his voice 'Form fours, my brave boys!' This was to mislead the enemy and gain a few precious moments of time. Meanwhile the Yankees began firing. They shot over our heads at first, but soon secured good range. The captain ordered the fence on our right pulled down so we could pass into a growth of timber. I sprang from my horse and lowered the fence. As the boys rushed through, one rode between me and my horse, and I was forced to turn him loose. The company kept right on and left me, striking the enemy's flank. Just then I wished that horse was somewhere else and I honorably with my wife and babies. Forty kingdoms would I have given for a horse, for my own little roan. I secured him with nerve, and just as I caught him I heard the hoof beat and muttering roar of Wharton's column as it advanced down the pike in a headlong charge 'rough riders' they were, sure enough."

October 4, 1862. L. S. Ferrell continues "Standing on his stirrups, bareheaded, his hair streaming behind, and whipping his gray mare Fanny across the withers with his hat, Gen. John Wharton (pictured) led the charge, shouting 'Charge 'em, boys!' I fell in with the Texans. When the head of our column struck the enemy the rail fence on our left went down in a moment, and we charged through an open woodland. Capturing a prisoner, Col. Tom Harrison ordered me to take him up behind me, and carry him to headquarters. As we had to retrace our steps and get on the pike to find headquarters, and as our forces had moved on and the Yankees were expected every minute, I thought it foolhardy to risk my prisoner with the advantage he would have behind me and for once disobeyed orders and made my prisoner doublequick. We had not proceeded very far when we encountered another Reb having charge of another prisoner. He asked me what I was going to do with my Yank. 'Take him to headquarters,' I replied. 'Yes, and we will both be captured. I'm going to kill mine right here,' he rejoined. At this the prisoner began begging for his life. I told Johnnie not to do so cowardly a deed as that, and requested him to turn his man over to me. 'Take him and go to [h]with him!' he shouted, and, putting spurs to his horse was quickly out of sight leaving me with both prisoners, who readily ran until we were out of danger."

Ferrill continues "By this headlong charge of Wharton's the Federals were scattered like chaff, and I think they lost about 15 in killed and wounded, and perhaps twenty five or thirty prisoners. We had but one man wounded and that was slight. After the battle of Perryville we rode into Stanford. As we drew up in front of the hotel there were a group of paroled Federals on the verandah. Soon one of them sprang up, exclaiming: 'Yonder's my man!' He ran to me and seizing my hand, seemed as glad as if he had found a long lost brother. He was one of the Bardstown prisoners."

OCTOBER 4, 1862. L.S. Ferrell's story goes on "On our way to the front we met one of the 8th Texas, who had a bullet hole in his forehead from which the blood flowed freely. He presented a ghastly sight to beginners. As he passed us, he pointed exultingly to his wound and wanted to know of Capt. Paul Anderson if that would not entitle him to a furlough." This was R. K. Cheatam, of Texas, who lived many years afterward carrying the bullet to his grave.

OCTOBER 4, 1862. Wheelers Cavalry was ordered to follow and cover the rear of the Left Wing of the army which was moving toward Glenville in Washington County. Converging on the country roads serving the farmers, the army vehicles and foot traffic churned up dust, then mud after the rain. Fords were used as well as the bridges. Hardee camped at Glenville and found "the dirt road since the rain very bad." Colonel Joseph Wheeler (pictured) was almost cut off by the Federals as he supervised the rear guard actions for Bragg's Army movement from Bardstown to Springfield. He waited until nearly dark then circled the town to avoid capture.

OCTOBER 5, 1862. Major Gen. Alexander McDowell, McCook's 1st Army USA camped at Bloomfield. Rev. Cunningham tells of his close call at Bloomfield. "I was walking in from Merrifield's when I was stopped by a picket in blue. I told him I wanted to go to my house in town. The first house I came to was that of Mrs. Joshua Gore. Mrs. Gore quickly rushed me upstairs, warning me that a correspondent of a New York Paper was in the house who had stated that the preacher was a widely known disloyal man and that if captured I was sure to be sent to prison at Camp Chase, Ohio. When the correspondent left the house, Mrs. Gore let me know the coast was clear. I hurried downstairs, out through the back hall door into the garden and soon found a place of seclusion, where I could see the Chaplin pike and see what was going on there, yet could not be seen from it."

OCTOBER 5, 1862. What Cunningham saw was, by his estimate, 15,000 infantrymen going toward Chaplin. These men made up the Union 1st Army Corps., commanded by General Alexander McCook (pictured), on their way to Perryville. They had spent Sunday around Bloomfield while McCook awaited orders on which way to send them. On Wednesday at Perryville they formed the Federal Left Wing and bore the brunt of the fighting. Two days after the preacher saw them on the Chaplin Road, 660 of them lay dead on the battlefield and 2,200 were wounded.

Major David McKee Claggett's diary entries tell what it was like to campaign with Rousseau's Division, McCooks Corps., of Buell's army through Nelson County on the way to Perryville. Pictured is a typical sutler's tent where you could buy everything from Bibles to whiskey.

October 3, 1862. "Stayed all day at Taylorsville. I went into town and found a relative, Samuel McKee, a rebel, but his wife was a good Union lady. Took tea with them, and when I got back to camp found the regiment ready to march. Went only two miles and camped for the night."

October 4, 1862. "Marched near noon for Bloomfield and camped there for the night. The Paymaster, Major Davis, paid the regiment off. Everyone had more money than they needed."

October 5, 1862. "This is Sunday and we remained in camp. About one half men and officers got drunk. There was some disturbance in the camp of the 21 Wisconsin Regiment on account of some runaway Negroes."

October 6, 1862. "Marched early and crossed the Chaplin River. We camped in the Chaplin Hills tonight."

October 7, 1862. "Marched at six o'clock and went to the town of Mackville and camped for the night. More pretty ladies and Union people here than I have ever seen since I have been in the Army. We hear some firing ahead a great battle is expected and the men are anxious for a fight."

October 8, 1862. "Our regiment is ordered back to Springfield with the division wagon train as a guard. Everyone is mad because we lost the chance for a fight. I don't say much as I am still sick. We march with the wagontrain to Springfield and go into camp. I am sent into town with two Captains to try and stop the vandalism of the stragglers from the army and treated with great courtesy by the citizens. Today the battle of Perryville is fought and Gen. James S. Jackson is killed."

Sister Marietta SCN remembers when the "saucy Yankees in blue invaded . . . they were the vanguard of Buell's army and were in hot pursuit of General Bragg. The boys in blue were very annoying, visiting the stable, dairy, etc, and pressing into service all they wished, were soon off. Mother Columba requested an officer to protect them from the insolence of these youths, but before discipline had been established, the soldier boys climbed on the outside of the window sills and taunted the girls who gave saucy retorts."

OCTOBER 4, 1862. All of the Confederate sick, except 60 extreme cases, were moved to Danville from St. Joseph' College. St. Joseph College was commandeered as a hospital by Col. Buell's troops in the evening. The sick Confederates were put under parole. OCTOBER 5, 1862. Buell's army passed through Bardstown, leaving 200 of his sick soldiers at the college hospital.

OCTOBER 5, 1862. First Lt. H. W. Reddick of Florida wrote of his experiences while in the hospital at Bardstown with a severe fever. He was still there when the Confederates evacuated Bardstown. "My room was on the third floor of the Female Academy which was used for a hospital and it fronted on the street so that I saw Buell's army as it passed through. I counted 110 flags. The wounded captured at Perryville were sent to the hospital at Bardstown and many of them died." The school mentioned did not have a full third floor but an attic space, probably with dormers, as so many of the buildings had before the advent of electricity. Pictured is a class of the 1890s at the front door.

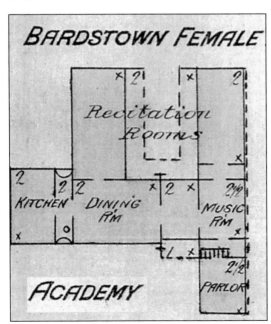

OCTOBER 5, 1862. Bardstown Female Academy was used by the Union troops as a hospital during the winter of 1862. The Confederates would utilize it during Bragg's occupation in September, 1862. This 1886 map indicates the north wings of the school and how the rooms were used. These wings were two-story brick with a wooden porch that connected the rooms with the main building. The wings were removed after 1910.

OCTOBER 5, 1862. General Buell and staff passed through Bardstown at half past eight in the morning. This picture shows Main Street as it appeared in the 1860s.

OCTOBER 6, 1862. McCook's two divisions (USA) settled down between the Chaplin River and Mt. Zion in Washington County.

OCTOBER 7, 1862. A message to Buell from J. B. Anderson read "I made an examination of the Bardstown road. The trestles are destroyed and it will require at least fifteen days to repair the road [the railroad]." Dumont to Army of the Ohio headquarters "Major portion of Gen. Bragg's forces passed up to Danville from Bardstown Friday last [4 days before] . . . Bragg's train of 600 wagons and upward of 30,000 troops, Infantry, Cavalry, and Artillery in due proportion."

OCTOBER 8, 1862. Federal Hill's windows reflected the thousands of Confederate and Union troops who traveled the Springfield Pike between 1861 and 1865. The widow Rebecca Rowan watched her oldest son, William, go off to join the Confederacy while William H. Lytle, cousin of the family, was a Colonel in the 10th Ohio and in charge of Camp Lytle Morton at Bardstown. Many of the local families were split in sympathies and allegiance.

OCTOBER 4, 1862. On that hot October day when the 15,000 troops and 600 wagon baggage train from Bragg's Army passed by the country stores, post offices, churches, and farmers' homes along the roads toward Springfield, people gathered to watch in wonder a spectacle which they never thought to see again. Unbeknownst to them, eight hours later the Union Troops of Buell's Army would travel down the same roads in greater numbers. This country store was about five miles east on the Springfield Pike at Botland, Kentucky.

OCTOBER 8, 1862. Bragg's army was spread out between Harrodsburg, Perryville, and Springfield, converging on Harrodsburg along several roads. At Perryville, while searching for water, the troops of Buell's following army suddenly came upon Confederates also stopping for water. The Yankees' force was 60,000 strong but spread over 20 miles. The Confederates had moved 15,000 from Bardstown with Kirby Smith's army of 25,000 from Lexington, also spread out over a wide area. The hilly terrain hampered intelligence about the battle and prevented the Commanders from knowing the actual numbers of the enemy. The Federals suffered more casualties (7,407) but the south's loss was more critical (3,196). Bragg's army won the battle but withdrew south into Tennessee.

OCTOBER 12, 1862. By this date, 50 additional Union soldiers were at the college hospital making a total of 310, 60 of whom were Confederate. The most difficult period of any during the war concerning St. Joseph College were the days between October 5 and 17. According to the book *Jesuits of the United States*, "There was much wrangling, at times even blows between the soldiers of North and South forced to live under the same roof. Some Union men who had feigned sickness so as to be left behind at Bardstown . . . drank and quarreled with one another, rode roughshod over all the hospital regulations, stole the college poultry and vegetables and invaded the private apartments of the fathers, the officers being unable to control them. A sigh of relief was breathed by the Jesuits when on October 17 some sixty or seventy of these undisciplined guests received their discharge from the hospital."

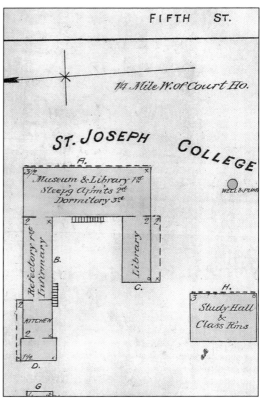

OCTOBER 15, 1862. Mother Columba mentions that the sisters are nursing in one hospital in Bardstown. First Lt. H. W. Reddick of Florida tells of his stay in the Bardstown hospital "We fared very well while our army was in Bardstown but after it was captured by the Yankees, things were bad indeed. While our army was there, the ladies visited us, and did everything they could for us, but when the Yankees came in, this was not allowed and if it had not been for the Sisters of Charity we would have fared much worse. They did everything they could for us, and I for one will never forget their kindness." It is estimated that more than 5,000 Union soldier "stragglers," thought to be mostly "new troops" from Buell's Army, came "thronging" through Bardstown. By order of General Buell, "twice a day, stragglers were pushed through Bardstown at the point of the bayonet by the provost guard."

OCTOBER 7, 1862. St. Thomas Church and Seminary was located about three miles south of Bardstown on the New Haven Pike. The Union camps of instruction in the winter of 1862 were one half mile away. Father Chambige, pastor at St. Thomas, was sympathetic to the South, but he treated the soldiers from both sides the same. His patience was tried when Federal soldiers surrounded the seminary and searched for a reported Southern soldier. When Bragg's Army left the area, Lieutenant Brown, son of Governor Brown of Georgia, and a private soldier from an Arkansas regiment, both sick of fever, were given shelter and care at the seminary. Buell's army replaced the Confederates at Bardstown and Lieutenant Kelly, of a Pennsylvania regiment, was sent to arrest the rebels. He found Lieutenant Brown too sick to be removed and he paroled him. Lieutenant Kelly, a Catholic graduate of Georgetown and son of Judge Kelly of Philadelphia, apologized for invading the quiet of the seminary; however, as a soldier, he had to obey his orders. Lieutenant Brown was seriously ill with typhoid fever and felt he owed his life to the nursing of Sister Ida of the Sisters of Charity. Before coming to the seminary, he had never seen a Catholic priest or sister. When he left, he presented Father Chambige with his horse and saddle, but unfortunately this was reported to the Union soldiers who confiscated them. Father Chambige did not view this as a proper action of war but as "highhanded robbery."

Three

AFTER PERRYVILLE-
MORGAN RIDES

OCTOBER 15, 1862. Morgan, after Perryville, had 1800 men—2nd Ky. Gano's and 3rd Ky. Breckinridge's Batt. He asked permission to find his own way home and went back into Central Kentucky. This picture represents Morgan's men at Paris, Kentucky, in July of 1862.

OCTOBER 17, 1862. The 78th and 91st Illinois Vol. Inf. arrived at New Haven to protect the railroad bridges and trestles.

OCTOBER 18, 1862. The bridge over the Rolling Fork destroyed by rebel forces has been repaired and trains are proceeding as far as Elizabethtown. Neither the trestlework nor the tunnel at Muldrough's Hill was damaged by the rebels.

OCTOBER 19, 1862. Morgan's men halted at Bloomfield for two hours to eat and rest. **OCTOBER 21, 1862.** The *Louisville Journal* reported "One of our local citizens, who was in Bloomfield yesterday . . . reported Morgan and a portion of his gang there . . . it is a scandal and a shame that he is uncaught. Morgan captured our few sick and wounded in Bloomfield, including three or four officers, and we presume he paroled them." Rev. John Cunningham writes: "A week or so after the battle of Perryville, October 8, General John H. Morgan with the body of his Cavalry entered Bloomfield in time to go into camp for a noonday meal. It was Sunday. I had preached at 11 o'clock at Beech Fork [pictured]. I was accustomed to preach once a month for the colored people on Sunday afternoons at Bloomfield, Beech Fork, Poplar Flat and Chaplin; but on account of the recent occupancy of that section by armies, I had no afternoon service that day at Beech Fork. I learned at the close of service that 'Morgan's men' were at Bloomfield and concluded I would go home. When I got there I found the town filled with Confederate Calvary and nearly ready to be on the move again. I had a nephew, Napoleon Bonaparte Lucas, from Bowling Green, with Morgan's troops. He had dined with his aunt and when I returned he was on his war steed, ready for the march before him. I found him and rode out of town with him. I met James Minor, borrowed a five dollar bill from him, gave it to my nephew and to that extent I helped the Confederacy. I rode with him to within a couple of miles of Bardstown and thence I went to the home of Governor Charles A. Wickliffe where I spent the night."

OCTOBER 20, 1862. Reverend Cunningham continues:"I left the Wickliffe mansion about 9 o'clock on Monday [October 20] morning and started homeward. At Arch Wilson's gate, several miles out, I met a long column of Union Calvary in pursuit of 'Morgan and his men.' I did not go far until I was stopped by a Captain who halted and interviewed me. He wanted to know if I was 'a loyal man.' I proposed to prove my 'loyalty' by Governor Wickliffe. He declared Governor Wickliffe disloyal and refused to take his endorsement. He ordered me to dismount from the large and substantial horse I was riding and directed a young fellow about twenty years old to dismount and take my horse. I meekly obeyed his order and the youthful soldier with signs of pleasure did as he was told to do. I was told to put my saddle on the unsaddled war horse of the soldier, which was a rather shabby looking animal to be in the Calvary service, and to bear the inscription on his person, 'U.S.' The Captain dismounted, transferred his military equipment to my horse and his war steed to the obedient young soldier. I mounted my new acquisition from Uncle Sam, and saw the Captain ride away in pursuit of 'Morgan and his men' on my horse."

OCTOBER 20, 1862. About nine o'clock at night, Company E of Morgan's Cavalry, led by Major Sale on a scouting expedition, captured and destroyed at Cox's Creek Bridge (pictured) a train of 160 wagons at camp. Some Confederate accounts say they captured "400 prisoners, six or seven hundred mules and large supplies, and a big Mail." Union accounts say "51 loaded (wagons) and 31 empty."

OCTOBER 21, 1862. The *Louisville Journal* reports Morgan's rebel cavalry were resting for a few hours at the fairgrounds near Bardstown. Having information about a wagon train carrying supplies to General Wood's Division at Crab Orchard camping at Cox's Creek, they or a portion of them pushed forward to Cox's Creek bridge where they encountered the train of 51 loaded and 31 empty wagons. The entire train fell an easy prey to the rebels. All the wagons were burned except three, which were driven off with government stores. The teamsters were marched out into the road and paroled. The horses and mules were driven away, except for those mules which wouldn't submit to the driving. They grazed in the vicinity of Cox's Creek bridge.

OCTOBER 22, 1862. Mother Columba of Nazareth Academy (pictured) reported the reopening of the mail. It was difficult to have it brought out; she sent a servant to get it, and while he was in the office his horse was taken away. Gov. Chas. A. Wickliffe employed Joseph Z. Aud to carry the US mail from Louisville to Bardstown after the railroad trestles were destroyed by Bragg's troops. Aud drove a two horse, six passenger stage which he said "sometimes carried up to 18 people, and was pulled by four horses." It was a triweekly mail. Wm. F. Graves and Ben F. Wilson ran a stage line between Bardstown and New Haven during the same period. When the railroad was repaired and reopened in late February 1863, both stage lines went out of business.

OCTOBER 26, 1862. A letter from Buell to Gen. Wright in Cincinnati read "If you have any more new troops, I suggest concentrating them in a camp of instruction at Bardstown, where they can be supplied and move in any direction by rail."

NOVEMBER 10, 1862. Mother Columba of Nazareth wrote "Soldiers of the regular army [68th Ind.] are stationed in town, and they are very different from the volunteers. The commander, Captain King, is much liked."

NOVEMBER 15, 1862. Mother Columba wrote "As long as our Sisters have been at the hospitals in town, arrangements have not been made to give them their meals. Had it not been for Mrs. B. Smith, they would have gone without."

DECEMBER 27, 1862. Bardstown City Marshall ordered to close the Negro Church (Church on Second Street) until further orders because of unrest.

DECEMBER 28, 1862. The Federals evacuated the town and took as many sick as could travel from the college hospital.

DECEMBER 29, 1862. General Morgan entered Bardstown and occupied the college hospital. They took prisoner and paroled the 150 federal soldiers left at the hospital.

Col. D. W. Chenault

Colonel Basil Duke

DECEMBER 1862. Morgan came into Kentucky in December on what is now called the Christmas Raid. He captured Elizabethtown and its Federal garrison on December 27. His real target was the trestles on the L & N railroad at Muldraugh's Hill. He captured and burned them on December 28. Raiding parties destroyed the Cane Run bridge and two bridges on the Lebanon branch. Morgan was determined to head south. He was encamped on the south bank of the Rolling Fork, still in Hardin County. The next morning most of the force crossed into Nelson County at a ford, a mile or two upriver from where the Elizabethtown-Bardstown Road crossed the river. Morgan sent Colonel Clukes' regiment with two pieces of artillery on an operation five miles downriver to destroy a railroad bridge over the Rolling Fork. Col. John Harlan and the federal troops caught up with Morgan's men and opened fire with artillery as they were crossing the ford. They sent for Cluke and determined to defend the fords until he could return or his force would be stranded. The rebels occupied a meadow which had a sort of terrace running across it. This protected the men, but not the horses. The rebels made a show of counterattacking, Cluke's regiment returned in good time, the Federals held back, and another good ford was discovered. The rebels escaped the trap. They lost as captured one captain, one sergeant and six privates. During the crossing of the river, Col. Basil Duke was wounded in the head by a bursting artillery shell. He fell into the river, but was rescued, placed in a wagon commandeered from a nearby house, and brought to Bardstown to be treated.

DECEMBER 29, 1862. Col. Basil Duke, second in command to Gen. J. H. Morgan, was wounded during a fight at the crossing of the Rolling Fork River near Lebanon Jct. and brought to Bardstown to be treated. Reverend Cunningham was on hand when Duke was brought to Bardstown, and stated "About dark Morgans men began to throng the streets. Among the arrivals was Col. Basil Duke of Morgan's Division of Cavalry. He had been wounded in the short battle whose cannons' roar we had heard. It was necessary for him to be helped by others into the hall of Dr. Cox's two story brick house (pictured) and up the stairway to the north end room, where he was laid on a thick pallet on the floor. Dr. Thomas Allen from nearby Taylorsville, a surgeon in Morgan's army, attended Col. Duke. I stood by and witnessed the treatment of the distinguished patient. The wound was on the right side of the head and when the doctor had washed the blood from it, I was invited to examine a cannon's work. The wound was supposed to be made by a small piece of bursted shell of a small cannon. A piece of the skin and bone behind the ear were gone. If the direction of the flying bit of shell had been directly from the right of the victim, it would have passed through the lower part of the head and death would have been instantaneous. As I bent over the prostrate warrior looking at his wound, he said in a somewhat cheerful tone, 'that was a pretty close call.' He did not complain or in any way indicate that his wound was a painful one."

December 30, 1862. Reverend Cunningham continues: "Early the next morning at the livery stable, I found my horse was gone and a 3 year old filly had been left in its place. I went to the neighboring hotel where I saw General Morgan on the sidewalk. I introduced myself and told him that my borrowed horse had been taken by one of his men. He promptly said 'You shall have your horse if he can be found. Go out on the Springfield Pike to a large white house on the left in the rear of which Col. Duke's command has been encamped. Wait there till our men are on the move. If you discover your horse, tell the rider you have my command for his surrender.' I left the courthouse square thronged with mounted warriors and rode out the Springfield Road two miles, when I came in front of the aforementioned white house, and there was my horse hitched to a post near the gate in the front yard."

December 30, 1862. "At the same time a soldier in gray came out and approached the horse. I said: 'Halt! That is my horse and I have the order for his restoration to me from Gen. Morgan.' He rode over the hill and stopped for a minute by some soldiers by a camp fire then dashed out of sight. I hitched my horse and walked down to the camp fire. I told the soldiers about my search for a lost horse. They laughed heartily, and when I told them seeing the rider of my horse ride out of my sight they laughed again. One man looked familiar to me, and when I asked him where he was from, he said Jefferson County, Ky. and his father was a prominent physician of that region. One man asked me to describe my horse. I did. Another asked 'Do you think you would know your horse if you should see him.?' I replied, 'I think I would.' More laughter 'Look at the horse behind you and see if it looks anything like yours.' I looked around and there was my horse within six feet of me. Then there was a general uproar of laughter from all. I looked again at the doctors son, 'You are the fellow that mounted my horse at the front gate.' He confessed he was and that he had galloped over the little hill and was back with his friends before I reached them. Seven years later I met a bridal party of several men and women from Jefferson County on an Ohio River steamer. I learned from one of them that he was a son of a Dr.____, had been a soldier in Morgan's command, was in Gen. Duke's brigade and at Bardstown in the Christmas raid. Then I said in a spirit of pleasantry: 'And you are the fellow that stole my horse.' This time the laughter was at his expense." The plantation house known as Culpeper is pictured.

DECEMBER 29, 1862. Colonel Chenault of Morgan's group destroyed the stockade of Boston and marched on to Bardstown. Pictured is a stockade on the L&N Railroad from *Harpers Weekly*. Morgan's men opened the county jail and freed several prisoners claiming to be Southern sympathizers accused of stealing horses. Others burglarized the post office. Stores were plundered when shopkeepers refused to take Confederate money.

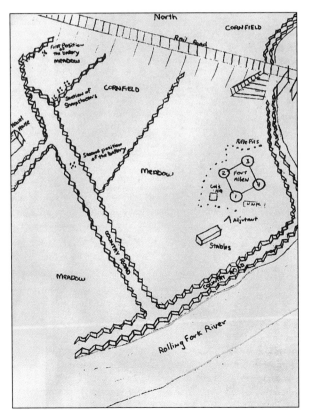

DECEMBER 30, 1862. Elements of Morgan's troops attacked the 78th Illinois Inf. USA, Col. Benneson at New Haven. The attack was driven off in a little more than 90 minutes. The stockade at New Haven, protected by about 80 infantrymen from Company H of the 78th Illinois, commanded by Col. William H. Benneson, had orders to stay strictly on the defensive and not to go more than 300 yards from the stockade. On the morning of December 30, they were approached by a flag of truce with a demand to surrender presented by the cavalrymen of Col. John H. Morgan, Captain Housley bearing the demand. Well prepared and with the advantage of position, Benneson "respectfully declined." The Confederates moved on the wooded ridge line to the northwest of the stockade and a single twelve pounder mountain howitzer was moved into position some 1,000 yards away in the meadow.

DECEMBER 30, 1862. Three companies of the Confederate 9th Kentucky Cavalry drew up into a battle line. The bombardment began but without much effectiveness. When the mounted men got closer to the action, they dismounted and hid their horses behind some buildings. The Federals put up a spirited defense and had the advantage of a well-prepared position. The exchange of shots was over in about 90 minutes with the Confederates withdrawing with 2 or 3 dead and 10 to 12 wounded. A 1918 newspaper article reported that the man who fired the Rebel howitzer was a New Haven native, Kit Owsley. None of his shots hit the stockade, but several rounds fell into the town. One of his shots struck the Farrill Building and another the Dawson House. Pictured is the main intersection with one of the business buildings in the background.

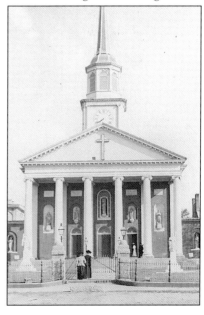

JANUARY 15, 1863. St. Joseph Cathedral, occupied by Union regiment of Tenn. Cav., was chosen in 1808 to be the seat of a diocese that would now include the states of Minnesota, Wisconsin, Michigan, Illinois, Indiana, Ohio, Kentucky, and Tennessee. St. Joseph Cathedral was constructed by 1819. The bishop moved the seat to Louisville in 1843, but this building continued to be important to the parish and the diocese as the first cathedral. The Jesuit fathers were in charge on January 15, 1863, when a Union regiment of Tennessee Cavalry asked permission to use the church as a barracks. "Not withstanding the protests of its pastors, the church was seized by them and occupied but for two days only." Folklore had the pastor sending for Judge John Newman, "the Union man" to come and deal with the soldiers. Judge Newman dropped enough names of generals to convince the soldiers to take care in how they treated the church. Two days later the regiment moved out of the church leaving it undamaged.

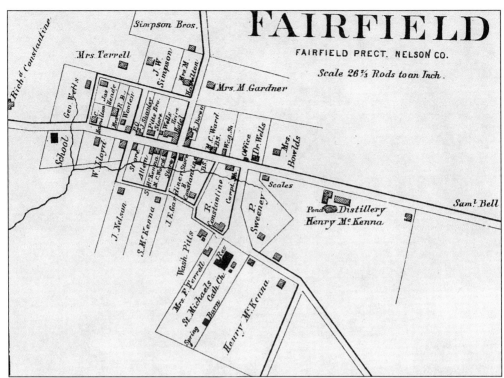

MARCH 1, 1863. The railroad from Bardstown to Louisville reopened after extensive repairs. The two stage lines were put out of business as shipping was restored to the community.

MARCH 3, 1863. Josephine Thomas of Bloomfield wrote "The government has stopped the mail to Bloomfield, I suppose because it is so disloyal or else because the guerrillas come there so much. But the people send to Fairfield every day or so and get their letters."

MARCH 6, 1863. "Direct my letter to Capt. Chas. Dawson ACS, 6th Ky. Regt. Helm's Brigade, Breckinridge's Division, Hardins Corps." were the directions given to Nancy Dawson by her father in a letter from Winchester, Tennessee, on March 6, 1863. He served in the famed "Orphan Brigade," so-called because it lost leader after leader during the war. Pictured is Charles Dawson's silver Masonic Medal worn by him during the war. On October 8, 1861, these Bloomfield men of Stone's Rifles of the Kentucky State Guard, Capt. Charles B. McClaskey, Lt. Charles Dawson, and 2nd Lt. Peyton Lee McMakin joined Co. A. Sixth Infantry CSA at Bowling Green.

JANUARY 1863. Mother Columba reports that the Sisters who had been nursing at Bardstown have returned. (Sisters Mary Ida Brophy and Mildred Travers are known to have nursed the soldiers at Bardstown but when is unknown.)

MARCH 27, 1863. The last 24 Union soldiers at the college hospital (pictured) were removed to Louisville.

MARCH 30, 1863. Mother Columba of Nazareth wrote "We have quite a number of Federal soldiers in town, a portion of Burnside's Army of the Potomac."

APRIL 30, 1863. The RRSB listed "Dr. Newman to Surgeon Myrlest, 1 car hospital stores 35 packages to Louisville."

MAY 2, 1863. Federal authorities return the college hospital to the Jesuits, everything clean and orderly "except for a few broken window panes."

MAY 5, 1863. The RRSB listed "Surgeon Newman to Surgeon Meylert 1 carload, (2) ambulances to Louisville."

MAY 28, 1863. The *Louisville Daily Journal* printed an article signed by a visitor to Bardstown. It indicated widespread southern sympathies in the town, and though "well protected at a vast expense to the United States ever since Bragg's army left, they indulge in hysterical hiding of their valuables whenever rumors indicate invasion by southern troops, miserable ingrates that they are." The smokehouses were used by citizens to hide their horses to keep soldiers from getting fresh mounts. Some even hid them upstairs in their homes. Blankets spread on the floor kept the sounds of the hooves from giving them away to visiting soldiers.

May 11, 1863. Capt. John C. Wickliffe's property was sold at the courthouse door while he was away with the 1st Kentucky CSA. Capt. Wickliffe and 1st Lt. George Schaub belonged to the Nelson Greys. They left September 24, 1861, and returned in 1865. In the spring of 1862, lawsuits were filed against Wickliffe and Schaub on notes and accounts due locals from the above soldiers. The following statement was in each petition "The defendant has left this the county of his residence and is cooperating with the army of the So Called Confederate States of America . . . during which period he has been and remained in the so called Confederate States or within their military lines."

On May 11, 1863, at the Courthouse door, commissioners exposed to sale J. C. Wickliffe's 38 acres of land and improvements, house in Chaplin, furniture, wagons, three slaves, tools, etc. to the amount of $3,647.80. All but $185.64 was used to pay notes and taxes. His father, Charles A. Wickliffe, purchased the 38 acres of land and brother-in-law W. N. Beckham purchased three slaves, some furniture including a cradle, while the rest went to townspeople. Lieutenant Schaub's "Sunken Garden" house (pictured) was spared by legal proceedings directed by his wife.

May 13, 1863. Union order #18 directed that the wives and families of Confederate soldiers be sent South. It was not generally enforced.

JULY 5, 1863. Pictured here is the Seven Star Tavern on North Third Street, half a block north of livery stable. Forty-five troops from Morgan's 1st Cavalry CSA surrounded 26 Federals from the Fourth US Cavalry in a livery stable at Bardstown. The skirmish lasted 20 hours, with the federals finally surrendering. Father Tom Major, who used to be known as Major Tom Major, recalled those times. "When Nelson County was reached Capt. Ralph Sheldon was put in charge of twelve picked men to do some scout work, and that he was one of those twelve men; that, when near the fairgrounds . . . they met twenty-six Union soldiers in the road; that they immediately fired upon the Yankees, and that the fire was quickly returned and a general fight ensued. The Yankees having twice as many men, compelled Sheldon's little squad to retreat, which they did in haste around the fairgrounds, through the Nazareth woods, and out by Hunter's Depot to the Shepherdsville road where they met some more of their men."

JULY 5, 1863. Then they rode into Bardstown, drove the Yankees into the Livery stable (pictured here with posters on the side) now owned by George Conner, and kept them there all night. The next morning the Yankees, 31 in number, under Captain Hynes, surrendered. Thirty of them were immediately paroled, but Captain Hynes, who had taken an oath never to take a Rebel soldier alive, was kept as a prisoner, and taken on to Shepherdsville. Father Major says as they went along down the Shepherdsville road, Hynes riding a horse to himself, that the Rebel who had him in charge got a little further behind the command the further they went. He says there was great enmity in the command towards Captain Hynes because of the oath of cruelty he had taken, and every man wanted the honor of shooting him. The man in charge of him fully intended to drop to the rear with him and kill him, but before this could be done, General Morgan learned that Hynes was in the rear in custody. His fears were aroused, and as Hynes had a brother who was a noble Confederate soldier, he determined to spare his life.

JULY 5, 1863. He galloped to the rear, rode up to Hynes and said "Mr. Hynes you are a free man, you are at liberty to go where you will." When General Morgan concluded, Hynes pointing to a Confederate said, "That fellow has my spur." General Morgan ordered the spur returned to Hynes, and rode back to the head of his command as Hynes returned to Bardstown. Father Major said that Morgan did not dignify Hynes by addressing him as Captain, but as Mr. Hynes, and showed his contempt by turning him loose without a parole.

Four

GUERRILLAS AND REPRISALS

JULY 6, 1863. Local lore has it that a bridge over the Beech Fork south of Bardstown was burned by Morgan while on his way to Ohio. The burning of the Beech Fork bridge between St. Thomas and Bardstown made it difficult for St. Thomas to obtain supplies. But Father Chambige kept St. Thomas open during these difficult times while other schools were closed or at half enrollment. The old fords were used until the bridge pictured above was built on the same site after the war.

July 25, 1863. A skirmish between New Hope and Rolling Fork Church (pictured) involved the Ohio 12th Cav.

July 27, 1863. Capt. Felix W. Graham of the 90th Ind. Cavalry wrote of chasing Morgan through the Nelson County area in the early part of Morgan's Ohio raid.

July 28, 1863. The Adjutant General's Report included the following: "Kentucky furnished 41,937 men to USA. Local counties Marion 735, Washington 738, Nelson 239, Spencer 91, and Hardin 386."

July 31, 1863. General Burnside declares martial Law in all Kentucky " . . . no disloyal person shall be allowed to vote." William F. Graves was appointed U.S. Provost Marshall. "I held the position right up to the close of the War. My headquarters were sometimes here [Bardstown], sometimes Springfield and sometimes Lebanon."

AUGUST 3, 1863. Col. Thomas H. Butler of the 5th Ind. Cav. erases the name of Charles A. Wickliffe from the poll book in his presence, and declares that no polling place in Kentucky is open to him even though he was a candidate for Governor. Thomas declares that Wickliffe is disloyal to the Union. Elections in Kentucky from 1799 until 1890 required the voter to come into the polling place and state his choice for the offices being elected. Several of the precincts in Nelson County received a written notice from the military commander of the county. "The judges, clerk and sheriff of District #5 in Nelson County met according to law and were served with an order form Lt. Col. Butler to allow no names to go on the Poll Books except a list furnished by Capt. Leeson, acting under the foregoing military order and we were further ordered by Capt. Leeson to proceed without the usual formality of an oath as required by the civil law. We therefore tender the foregoing report containing a list of the votes cast for the different candidates mentioned by the hands of Capt. Leeson to the clerk of the county court for the action of the proper officers. R. E. Horrell, Clerk." So read the report of the election officers in the August 3rd election.

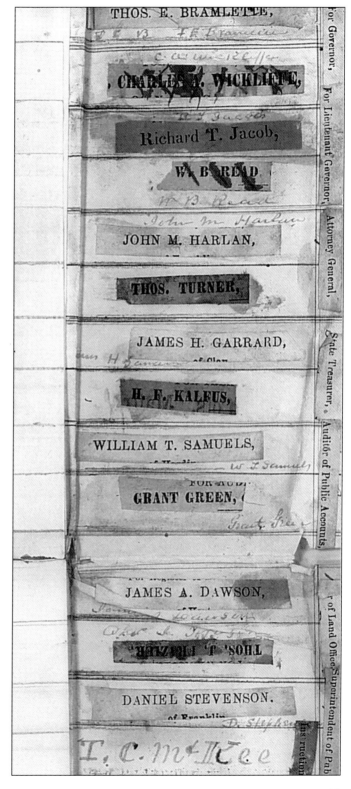

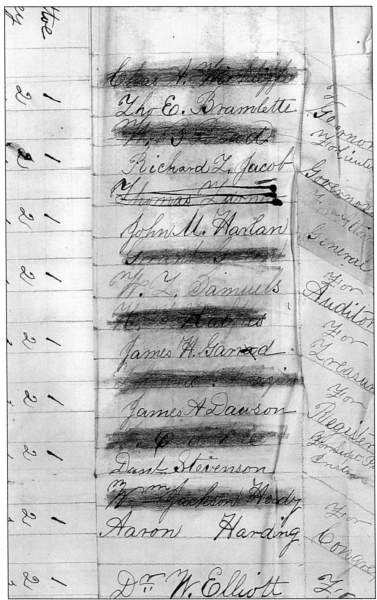

AUGUST 3, 1863. A statement attached to the Poll Books read "C. S. Wickliffe protests against the act by which his name was stricken from the POLL BOOKS and the people denied the privilege of voting for him as a candidate for the office of Governor. He states that he has always been opposed to Secession or deportation of the Union. He is in favor of a restoration of the Union as it was under the Present Constitution. He has opposed the abolition of Slavery as a war measure and the Armies of Negroes as soldiers of the army of the United States, and voted against the Appropriation Bill at the last session after the House refused to adopt the proviso offered by Mr. Mallony providing in substance that no part of the money should be expended in freeing Negroes, in arming and paying Negroes as soldiers of the Army. Mr. Crittenden, Mr. Maloney, Mr. Munsey, Mr. Hardin, Mr. Yeaman, Mr. Grider opposed the Bill and refused to vote for it for the same reasons. I deny that I am disloyal to the Government and the Constitution. I request the judges to file this paper with the Poll book and returns. C. A. Wickliffe."

AUGUST 3, 1863. The *Louisville Democrat* tried to report about these suppressed votes, but the Union controlled the press in Louisville and made fun of these statements, "Possibly an officer of the polls here and there may have mistaken his duty, but we are very sure that no votes worth mentioning, which ought to have been received, were rejected." When Governor Wickliffe complained to the public through the *Louisville Journal*, their reaction was "stop whining." Their investigation indicated "they had never saw an election more free from all military interposition and more open to voters of all parties." *Collins History* notes differently that " . . . only about 85,000 out of 140,000 votes polled . . . probably 40,000 being refused a vote, or kept from the polls by military intimidation or interference or by threats of arrest . . . regular Union candidates elected over the "Independent Union" and over the Democratic candidates in every case."

The main street of Bardstown, looking north from the court square in this 1900 photograph looks much as it did in 1862 when Bragg's and Buell's armies marched through the streets. Remove the telephone poles and the automobile on the lower right and the spire of the Christian Church on the upper right and the picture moves back thirty-five years. Replace one building on the right, add ninety-nine years and the street is as it appears today.

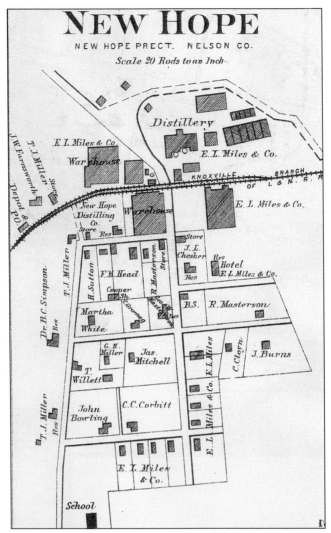

NEW HOPE

NEW HOPE PRECT. NELSON CO.

Scale 20 Rods to an Inch

OCTOBER 8, 1863. Richardson's guerrillas surprise and destroy a train at New Hope, Nelson County, and tear up the tracks.

OCTOBER 9, 1863. The *Louisville Journal* reports "Yesterday Afternoon, about 2 o'clock, the Louisville-bound train on the Lebanon Branch of the Louisville and Nashville Railroad was captured at New Hope, twenty miles from the junction, by that celebrated bushwhacker, Capt. Richardson. The road was so obstructed by the rebels as to throw the train off the track, and after it had run off they fired into it, causing the utmost consternation among the passengers. Richardson then made a demand for the surrender of the train. In the helpless condition of the passengers, they could do nothing more than yield to his demand. After the surrender, however, all the passengers were robbed of their clothing, money, and other valuables, the cars were all set on fire and destroyed, the locomotive disabled, and the track torn up for a short distance. The utmost indignity was offered the passengers, and outrages were perpetrated of that stealing, cutthroat character which characterize these scions of the chivalry. The locomotive was so disabled as to be rendered useless without the most expensive repairs. We have not learned the number of passengers on the captured train. We understand, however, they were all paroled and allowed to depart most of them minus coats, boots, money, etc. After doing all the damage they could, the rebels left in the direction of Lebanon."

OCTOBER 17, 1863. Twenty six of Gen. John H. Morgan's men escape from Camp Douglas in Chicago by digging under the fence from one of the barracks. **NOVEMBER 28, 1863**. Gen. John H. Morgan and six captains escape the Ohio Penitentiary at Columbus.

In an article in the magazine *Confederate Veteran* on December 17, 1903, Dr. R. H. Peak, the only survivor of the party who was captured with General John H. Morgan and escaped from the Ohio penitentiary, writes interestingly of that escape. "I was captured when General Morgan surrendered in Ohio; 365 of us surrendering with the General were carried to Camp Chase and confined there four weeks. On the way from Camp Chase to Camp Douglass on the 26th of August, I escaped from the cars and walked from there to Boone County, Kentucky. I passed through Kentucky, stopping for a short rest at Bardstown, the home of Capt. Sheldon, a comrade. After leaving Bardstown I went to lower Tennessee." Camp Chase was located in Columbus, Ohio. Pictured here is Capt. Ralph Sheldon.

DECEMBER 3, 1863. Gen. John H. Morgan and Capt. Thomas Hines spent the night "in the vicinity of Bardstown" after escaping from the Ohio Penitentiary. Some claim they stayed at the William Johnson house in Bardstown, but with Federal troops occupying Bardstown they would have avoided known Southern supporters. In later years, it was reported that they had stayed at St. Thomas. That report may be backed up by the account given below of one night at Holy Cross, a church further south, just across the Marion County line. Father David Russell wrote in 1929 about a story he had heard from Father Wuyts who was at Holy Cross at the time.

"A good woman employed as cook had just served supper to the three priests, when a cautious knock was heard at the door. Father Smarius, being nearest to the door, opened it and invited the stranger to come in. The man said at once in an undertone, 'You do not know me, but I know you are Catholic Priests who will not betray us. General Morgan and I have succeeded in escaping from the Ohio penitentiary and we are making our way to the South guided from friend to friend on our way. Here, we know no one and we are weary and hungry.' Of course he was invited to come in. Gen. Morgan and Capt. Hines shared the plain but ample supper with the priests, sat with them and narrated incidents of their perilous journey, then left to proceed on their way through the night. Morgan's companion was one of his officers whose name Father Russell does not recall." Hines notes they stayed at "Mr. McCormack's at Rolling Fork creek in Nelson County" on December 4, 1863.

DECEMBER 1863. The 33rd Ky. Inf. replaced the Indiana troops at New Haven. They remained until February 1864.

JANUARY 18, 1864. The distillation of corn in Kentucky is prohibited by Military general orders, but was revoked on February 14.

FEBRUARY 12, 1864. A claim was made for payment of two bridges burned on the Louisville-Bardstown Turnpike by order of General Nelson to delay General Bragg's Confederate forces in 1862.

MARCH 28, 1864. A skirmish at New Hope involved the 52nd Ky. Inf. USA.

FEBRUARY 20, 1864. The railway accident on the L& N railroad near Lebanon Jct. was due to the increasingly cold weather on the iron rails which, becoming filled with frost, are made brittle and easily broken. Railway employees are said to avoid riding the cars when it is so cold. The *Harper Weekly* drawing of the accident in pictured.

March 24, 1864. "Camp Butler, near Springfield Ill. Barracks # 18, Mr. Jonathan Hibbs, Sir: Your son, William is here a prisoner of war & sick with the measels. Being a fellow prisoner and a member of the same company, I felt it my duty to inform you of the fact, and place myself at your service. I shall do all in my powr to alleviate the sufferings of your son during his sickness. He is now in the hospital & as well taken care of as the means will admit. Though a prisoner & sick, he has friends. If I can be of any service further write to me. If William should get any worse I shall inform you. You need not be uneasy at present as he is mending. With much respect, I am Your & etc. G. C. Harris Prisoner of War Co. G. Clukes' Regiment"

William Hibbs joined the 8th Ky. at Bardstown in September 1862. He was captured on the Ohio raid with Morgan in August 1863. During the six-hour period Morgan's group was in Bardstown, William went home to visit his family in the Samuels area. He took them this Parker Snow 1863 rifle he had captured from a Union soldier. It was a treasured souvenir of the conflict because on March 28, 1864, this letter was received. "To: Jonathan Hibbs, Your son William died this morning, his body is at your disposal. G. C. Harris."

June 17, 1864. Col. George M. Jessee CSA with 150 mounted "Jessee's Riflemen" camped between Bloomfield and Bardstown and was thought to have been with Morgan at Cynthiana. Five or so men from Jessee's camp went to the home of John R. Jones (pictured) near Bloomfield. They demanded a horse, saddle, and bridle from him. He refused and shot one of the soldiers. They returned the fire, killing him.

June 18, 1864. Two union groups set out to capture Jessee, but Lieutenant Driskell surrendered his group without a fight. His surrender was much to the dismay of Major Smith of the 9th Mich., who arrived too late to assist him.

July 5, 1864. Lincoln suspends writ of Habeas corpus and proclaims martial law in the state.

August 2, 1864. Capt. J. B. Nipp of Co. C of the 40th Ky. Mounted Inf. USA attacked a Confederate camp in New Haven and captured seven prisoners. Two prisoners were shot trying to escape. An August 1864 *Louisville Journal* clipping reported "Affairs at Bloomfield—One battery of the 35th Kentucky Mounted infantry, under the command of Major Bristow, is now stationed at Bloomfield, in Nelson County. Bristow's men of the 35th are good soldiers and very gentlemanly in their deportment toward the citizens. The guerrillas had better give Bloomfield a wide berth hereafter. Major Bristow's men have had considerable experience in guerrilla hunting and as a general thing they have been very successful." Dr. Merrifield, local historian of Bloomfield, notes that they were camping at Miss Sallie Stone's.

Bloomfield Aug. 14th 1864

Dear Pa

  I am to be executed in a few moments, I do not want you, ma & the children to grieve after me; bear it with as much fortitude as possible. I think I am prepared to die. I have been living as a christian ever since I have been in prison, reading my testament & praying so don't grieve for my sake assure yourself that I am prepared & not scared,

    Your son

     R. Berry

AUGUST 14, 1864. When Confederate prisoner Richmond Berry was told that he was to be executed for the shooting of local farmer James Jones by members of Jessee's Regiment, he asked if he could write to his family. Pictured is a handwritten copy of his letter which was found in a family album. It appears to have been written in a woman's hand.

AUGUST 14, 1864. John May Hamilton and Richmond Berry were brought to Bloomfield to be executed in punishment for the killing of John R. Jones by Confederate troops in June. Brought from a prisoner of war camp in Lexington, where they had been imprisoned accused of being guerrillas, Hamilton and Berry were not aware of their fate until shortly before the execution. The younger Berry wrote a letter to his mother while walking to the place chosen for the execution. He showed signs of weakness and was told by Hamilton to "die brave." The people of Bloomfield placed their bodies in metal caskets laid out in the Masonic Hall. Local citizens grieved over these men, punished in retaliation for another's crime. Berry's family claimed his body, but Hamilton was buried in Bloomfield Maple Grove Cemetery. Major Bristow's 35th Kentucky Mounted Infantry supplied the firing squad. John Terrell was said to be one of only a half dozen or so Unionists in Bloomfield, yet he was a successful merchant there for many years afterwards. Obviously his rebel neighbors didn't boycott him. For one thing, he was credited with saving Bloomfield when a Union commander wanted to burn it down.

August 26, 1864. In 1861, the Venerable Charles A. Wickliffe of Bardstown had been a Unionist leader in soliciting the shipment of the "Lincoln rifles" to Kentucky, and in the action necessary to see that they got into the hands of Kentuckians loyal to the Union. Here are the words of this same man at the Democratic Convention in Chicago, the last week of August 1864: "Many of the best and most loyal citizens of Kentucky among them 20 or 30 ladies are now imprisoned by the military in Louisville, in damp and dirty cells, with only straw to lie upon, and the coarsest fare. The newspapers of Louisville are forbidden to make the slightest allusion to this terrible state of affairs. I proclaim it here and now at the risk of my liberty, perhaps of my life."

August 26, 1864. Julia Wickliffe Beckham had heart-wrenching experiences during the war. Her father, Ex-Gov. C. A. Wickliffe was a staunch Unionist, but her brother John C. Wickliffe had joined the 5th Kentucky in September 1861. A family story tells of her answering a knock on the side door of the home (pictured above) and receiving a letter from John by a Confederate soldier, when a loud knock on the front door was a Union soldier asking to search the grounds for a reported "reb."
August 27, 1864. Mother Colomba of Nazareth writes "a Negro regiment has been stationed near Bardstown for about two weeks. They are quiet as far as I know."

97

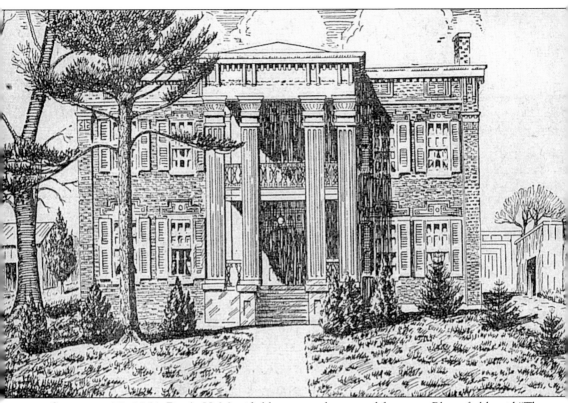

September 19, 1864. Dr. A. H. Merrifield, a young doctor and farmer at Bloomfield, said "The tightest place I ever was during the war was when I was drafted and had to appear before that august tribunal at Lebanon made up Fidler and Maxwell. I thought by some hook or crook or by some scheming I could get off, but my plans were not worth a cent and I was given to understand that they had heard of me. So I had to go into the army or furnish a substitute and had but a short time to procure one. Fortunately, everybody in Lebanon knew my father. I went to a merchant, a great friend of his, and told him my condition, who I was, and then the amount of money I wished, which was $600. In reply he said, 'If you are Col. Merrifield's son, you can not only get $600, but $6000 if necessary.' So I went to the barracks where the Negroes were being sold, and bought one of Col. Horace Stone's Negroes for $600. There had been in the neighborhoods of Bloomfield, Fairfield, and Chaplin, Federal soldiers whose business it was to press in Negroes and sell them at Lebanon as substitutes." Fidler was the provost marshal. The Merrifield home "Walnut Grove" is pictured here.

SEPTEMBER 19, 1864. William Carothers of Bardstown received the coded message that he had been drafted in the Union Army. His brother was in the Confederate army, and he was determined to escape Kentucky and the draft. His journal details his experiences of avoiding the Union draft. On September 18, a draft was held at Lebanon. He directed his friend to notify him by telegraph if he was drafted to send, "You are not drafted." "Mr. White the telegraph operator came to my house at midnight. I was sleeping over Baker Smiths' Store where I was employed and when he knocked I looked out the window. 'I have good news for you, You are not drafted.' With a sinking heart I hastily dressed and went home packed my trunk and had it sent to Nazareth [depot] and kissing my mother and sisters goodbye and promising to write, I hastened to the depot to catch the morning train for Louisville. Took on my trunk at Nazareth and at half past eight reached Louisville in safety. I visited the rooms for substitutes and found I couldn't get one for less than $2,500 which I thought was excessive and I didn't have the money. I exchanged my greenbacks into gold and purchased a ticket from Jeffersonville to New York." Adventures crossing the Ohio, catching the train, and avoiding the military checking passes brought him to New York. He looked up Rev. Nathan L. Rice, the former president of Roseland Academy who was the Carothers' next door neighbor at Bardstown. He was then the pastor of the Brick Presbyterian church, "the wealthiest church in the United States." On October 15, he took Dr. Rice's advice and left New York for Canada. Dr. Rice accompanied him to the railroad station and gave him ten dollars in gold saying, "it was done for the love of my parents and for my good luck." James Carothers' house is pictured here.

These two entries were taken from Carothers' (pictured above) journal.

OCTOBER 20, 1864. "got a job with an 'old Frenchman dairy farmer' who offered to pay fourteen dollars a month to milk for him. Stuck it out for three weeks then went back to job searching." Locating a man who resembled him in appearance, Carothers proposed to have him, William Marcus Butler, take out papers for the United States. Carothers obtained a certificate as British subject, William Marcus Butler, and under this name, crossed over the border traveling to Pennsylvania.

NOVEMBER 15, 1864. At the home of his father's brother Abraham, Carothers wrote "Visiting around [his] relatives and helping on the different farms took up most of the time until January. Went to prayer meeting, tried to get a job on the Pennsylvania Railroad, searching the newspaper ads for positions." Discouraged and far from home he wrote: "I was greatly surprised at receiving a letter from home with my dear mother's ambrotype . . . the image is not equal to the original." He traveled to Philadelphia in January trying to find work, had his money stolen from his trunk, and worked as a streetcar conductor until some soldiers tried to shoot him for putting them off the car. He also worked in the repair shop at the streetcar company. When applying for a job, he was asked if he was a Presbyterian. He presented a letter from "Rev. Joe McDonald, the blind preacher," who called him "his elder" as a reference for a government job. On February 1st, he went to Washington for work. He returned home after the war and entered into business with his brother who also survived the war.

SEPTEMBER 22, 1864. Eleven guerrillas led by Henry Magruder unsuccessfully attacked the train a short distance from New Haven. Continuing to New Haven, they burned the railroad depot to the ground. Pictured is the depot which replaced the one destroyed.

SEPTEMBER 23, 1864. The *Louisville Journal* reported "Destruction of the New Haven Depot. A party of eleven mounted guerrillas, under the command of the notorious Magruder, attacked the up train over the Lebanon Branch Railroad yesterday, a short distance from New Haven, the train guard gallantly returned the fire and handsomely repulsed the guerrillas. It is reported that two of the scoundrels were killed and one or two wounded. The train passed on to Lebanon and the outlaws started for New Haven, entered the place without resistance, and in the presence of a large number of the male citizens applied the torch to the railroad depot building and guarded it until it was burned to the ground. The citizens of New Haven exhibited little spirit in permitting a handful of outlaws to thus destroy one of the public buildings of the town. The train returned safely over the road from Lebanon in the evening, the thieves having abandoned the line."

SEPTEMBER 22, 1864. Coming directly from New Haven, where they had burned the Depot, "Henry Magruder and eight of his guerrillas are in Bardstown where they captured the telegraph operator, demolished his instrument and stole his personal effects. They intended to burn the Depot, but were treated to some 'fine old whiskey, and a present of some jars of delicious pickles' by the railroad agent and went away without damaging the building. No attempt was made by the citizens of Bardstown to capture these men."

SEPTEMBER 23, 1864. Magruder's band were in New Hope where they robbed the citizens and waited in ambush for the "up" train. Learning that it was strongly guarded, Magruder wisely withdrew. He was still a threat to the bridge over the Rolling Fork. NOVEMBER 7, 1864. Three men, Hopkins, Sipple, Stagdale, supposed to be guerrillas, were shot to death seven miles from Bloomfield in retaliation for killing of two Negroes by Sue Mundy's men. This is a separate execution from the next story, although close to the same time.

Pictured is an 1859 map of the area around Nelson County which had frequent guerrilla activity. The guerrillas were familiar with the roads and where they could hide out or "lay low." Many different bands were operating in late 1863 and 1864. Some reports had the same band in two different locations and with different leaders. Information was as difficult to confirm as the guerrillas were to catch.

NOVEMBER 5, 1864. The 37th Ky. at Bardstown reported on the attack on guerrillas at Bloomfield. The message went out to Union headquarters in Kentucky from the officer commanding the 37th Ky. at Bardstown on November 7, 1864: "I have the honor to report to you that on the 5th instant as one of my companies entered Bloomfield, under command of Capt. Borrell, they surprised a lot of guerrillas at that place, 15 in number, who where having their horses shod, and had been pillaging the town. Three guerrillas were captured and two badly wounded, said to be mortally; the two wounded men made their escape. On the following day the Captain started the three to me at this place, and about 5 miles, he states, from Bloomfield, they tried to escape, and all of them were killed by their guards. Their remains were carried to Bloomfield the following day [or on the 6th instant] by citizens, who gave their names as follows: Tindle, Parkhurst, alias Jack Rabet, and Warford. The notorious Sue Mundy and Berry are said to be the ones who were wounded and made their escape. Berry is now reported dead; that he died the day after the fight in Fairfield. I have sent there for information." Historian Merrifield says the men were named Tom Hurst, Tingle, and Warford. Pictured here is the Durrett home on the corner of Main and Perry Streets in Bloomfield.

November 1864. W. J. Nelson wrote in *The Kentucky Standard* in 1938 of his knowledge of the Guerrillas: "In the fall of 1864, One Arm Berry assembled about 300 of his men in the streets of Fairfield, and marched on three roads to Bardstown and attacked a garrison of federal troops barricaded in the courthouse (pictured on the left). After some maneuvering, they surrounded the garrison and opened the fight. They were repulsed, several killed and many wounded, among them was One Arm Berry shot through." Taken to a private home near Fairfield, he was secretly treated and slowly recovered.

November 12, 1864. The Bloomfield Baptist Church minutes read "No meeting on account of soldiers presence having had a slight skirmish this morning."

November 25, 1864. The Presbyterian minister of Bloomfield bravely performed the service over Private Charles Augustus Lewis of the 1st Reg. Cav. CSA when his body was returned to be buried. The fear of Federal reprisal was high in Bloomfield in 1864. Confederate soldier Charles Augustus Lewis was killed at Glasgow by the Home Guard while returning home. After his family finally succeeded in obtaining his body, the local preachers were afraid to conduct his funeral. Reverend Sanders, pastor of the Presbyterian church, said he was not afraid, and Lewis was finally buried at the Lewis Cemetery at Bloomfield.

December 6, 1864. Burr Edward Coomes was mustered in the Union Army in the 10th Ky. Vol. Infantry in Lebanon, Kentucky, on November 21, 1861; he was mustered out in Louisville on December 6, 1864. Pictured is the mustering out picture of Company E three days later. He settled in Nelson County after marrying Nora Moore.

December 21, 1864. Congress passed a law to tax all whiskey manufactured after January 1, 1865, at $2 per gallon.

DECEMBER 29, 1864. The 7th Penn. Cavalry under Colonel Minty marched two miles beyond Bardstown to the camp of the 3rd Ohio that had remained at that place. They were on their way to Nashville. Two officers of the 7th PA Cavalry were attacked and murdered by Guerrillas at the home of W. R. Grigsby (pictured) on the Springfield Pike near Bardstown. The *Pottsville Miners Journal* (PA) reported on January 14 "On Thursday afternoon, while the Seventh Pennsylvania cavalry were approaching Bardstown, Ky., Capt. R. McCormick, AAG on the colonel's staff and Major John L. Shirk, Surgeon of the regiment, went into the house of a Mr. Grigsby, one mile out of town. Major Shirk was acquainted with the family, and not having seen them for some time concluded to pay them a friendly visit."

DECEMBER 29, 1864. The *Pottsville Miners Journal* article continues "They had been there but a few minutes, and Mr. Grigsby's daughter was entertaining them with a song at the piano. A negro woman rushed into the room, but upon seeing the officers she rushed out again. Miss G. followed her out, but she came back hurriedly, and before she could tell the officers of the danger they were in, the house was surrounded by Sue Mundy and fifteen guerrillas. The guerrillas fired upon them through the window and doors, but did not succeed in hitting either of them. Mr. G. went to the door and informed the guerrillas that there were but two soldiers in his house, and that they would surrender. They pushed him to one side, rushed in, and murdered both of them on the spot." Congressman Ben Johnson wrote several local history columns in the 1930s, this is his version of the attack. "Babe Hunter and twelve or fifteen other guerrillas were coming from Marion County to Bardstown when at the top of Pottershop Hill they looked across the valley at the Grigsby residence a few hundred yards away. They saw several Yankee officers enter the residence. They had called to pay a visit to the Grigsby family but more particularly to Miss Ella Grigsby. The Guerrillas galloped over, surrounded the residence, went in and killed the officers. The Federals made hot pursuit but failed to capture Hunter or any of his men." Major Charles McCormick, pictured, escorted his brother's body home from Louisville.

JANUARY 17, 1865. A letter received at Nazareth read "Miss Columba Carroll, Mother Superior of Nazareth, Bardstown, Ky. My dear Madam, I received your letter of the 9th Inst. two days ago. I called on the President this morning, and presented your case for his consideration. He promptly gave me a safeguard which I enclose herewith which I hope will protect you from further depredations. It afforded me pleasure to serve you in this matter. If I can serve you further command me. I have the honor to be Your ob't serv't L. W. Powell."

The pictured safeguard reads " Let no depredation be committed on the property or possessions of the 'Sisters of Charity' at Nazareth Academy, near Bardstown, Ky. Jan. 17, 1865. A. Loncoln."

January 18, 1865. Capt. Edwin Terell and 13 men had a desperate fight with guerrillas, killing three near New Haven.

January 27, 1865. Five guerrillas with "One-Arm Berry" (pictured) hold 30 Federal soldiers in check for 20 minutes near Bardstown.

January 31, 1865. The *Louisville Daily Journal* reported "Guerrilla fight at Bardstown— Berry killed—fourteen soldiers murdered at Bloomfield—On Friday afternoon last, a squad of guerrillas, with the notorious Capt. Berry at their head, approached to within a short distance of Bardstown, where they were met by a party of Federal soldiers and fired upon. The outlaws stood their ground and boldly returned the fire, keeping the soldiers at bay for about 20 minutes. Our men outnumbered the guerrillas six to one, yet they suffered themselves to be held in check and at last permitted the scoundrels to escape. It is stated that Berry [the one-armed desperado] was shot and killed in the skirmish. On Saturday evening a gang of outlaws made another raid on the place, but after a brisk fight they were repulsed."

JANUARY 17, 1865. A letter from George W. Hite, Bardstown Unionist, to the Federal authorities, read "Do not forsake us and give us up to guerrillas. We will have no force here in a few hours. Company A of the 35th is the only force here and it is ordered to Lexington. Let this Co. remain here if possible. If they must go give us protection forthwith."

JANUARY 28, 1865. Eighteen Home Guards were busy plundering the stores of Bloomfield (pictured) when they were attacked by a force of about 60 led by Capt. Jerome Clark. In the skirmish, 17 of the Home Guards were killed. The *Louisville Daily Journal* reported "On Saturday Sue Mundy's band of Guerrillas made a dash into Bloomfield, surprised a party of seventeen discharged soldiers, captured fourteen of them and shot them to death on the spot. We were unable to learn to what command they belonged. A few days before the perpetration of this bloody outrage, the soldiers had captured and executed a guerrilla named Dudley, which prompted Sue Mundy and her cutthroats to retaliate in such a barbarous manner." The newspaper continued to refer to Jerome Clark, also known as Sue Mundy, as a female, after there was evidence to the contrary. In many areas the Home Guards were as much a threat to the citizens as the guerrillas. Personal feuds and retaliations were the excuses for many of the outrages by the Guards.

JANUARY 30, 1865. The Official Military Report read "Captain Searcy [of the 30th Ky. Inf. Union] had a running fight with Clarke's guerrillas three miles east of Chaplintown last Monday; wounded one of them; had better horses, got away. Captain came to Bloomfield on Tuesday; Fifty-fourth [Union] run in on him had a fight, wounding one man, killed a horse, before learning who they were."

FEBRUARY 1, 1865. In Missouri, Olivia Dawson Cooper was very outspoken about her support of the Confederacy. While her husband Zack was away in the Southern Army, her Federalist neighbors ordered her to leave the area. When she didn't, they burned her home. She fled to Waverly, Missouri, until she could find a way to come to Kentucky. After a three month stay, family history says that Quantrill and his riders escorted her and her three children back to Kentucky. When the Cooper family returned to Lee's Summit, Missouri, after the war, all that they found at their homestead were "the chimney and the jonquils blooming," the jonquils from bulbs she had taken from Hungry Run many years before.

FEBRUARY 26, 1865. A memento of Quantrill was long in the possession of a lady at Bloomfield—a poem written in an autograph album. The album belongs to Miss Nancy Dawson and the poem was written at her request when Quantrill was a guest in her father's house, Hungry Run, pictured above.

My horse is at the door.
And the foe I soon may see,
But before I go, Miss Nannie
Here's a double health to thee.
Here's a sigh for those who love me,
And a smile for those who hate.
And whatever sky's above me,
Here's a heart for every fate.

Though the cannons roar about me:
Yet it still shall bear me on,
Though dark clouds are above me,
It hath springs which may be won.
In this verse, as with the wine
The libation I would pour,
Should be peace with thine and mine,
And a health to all indoor.

Feb. 26, 1865 W.C.Q.

It is based on another poem by Byron "My Boat is on The Shore."

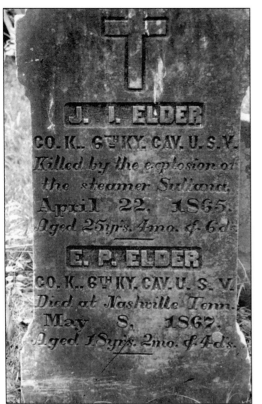

APRIL 5, 1865. Josephine Thomas wrote in a letter, "The guerrillas still infest Bloomfield and vicinity. The Yanks gobble one of them up occasionally. They had a fight near there the other day and killed three Yanks. The same or next day they caught another Yank and brought him near there and hung him in retaliation."

APRIL 9, 1865. The war is over.

APRIL 28, 1865. John I. Elder, Co. K. Sixth Ky. Cav. USV, was killed by the explosion of the steamer *Sultana*. "April 22, 1865, Aged 25 years, 4 mos. & 6 d.," in St. Michael's Cemetery at Fairfield, the tombstone of John I. Elder tells the sad tale of a returning Union soldier losing his life after the war was over. Elder had been captured on April 6, was exchanged, and was on his way to Louisville and home when he died. His brother, who was in the same unit, died two years later in the hospital at Nashville. (The tombstone death date and the historical account do not agree. The carving of the tombstone at a later date may explain the confusion. Both sons' deaths were inscribed on the back of their father's tombstone.)

APRIL 27, 1865. One day after this picture was taken, in the darkness of the night, the boiler of the steamer *Sultana* exploded, sinking the ship and 1200 returning Federal soldiers just released from the southern prison camps.

Five

AFTERMATH

JUNE 5, 1865. A letter written by Josephine Thomas at Bloomfield reads "I believe the guerrillas are about played out in this country. They have all been killed or surrendered or almost all. We take no paper and I do not know what is going on in the political world. If things go on as they have indeed I don't want to know much." Quantrill's sash (pictured) was a spoil of the war. Captured by Quantrill from Colonel Bloun near Lexington, Missouri, Quantrill is said to have worn it ever since. It became the property of Frank James who gave it to Donnie Pence, whose widow gave it to Ben Johnson. Made of silk, it is ornamented with large tassels. Some think the stains on it are from the last wounds suffered by Quantrill at Wakefield.

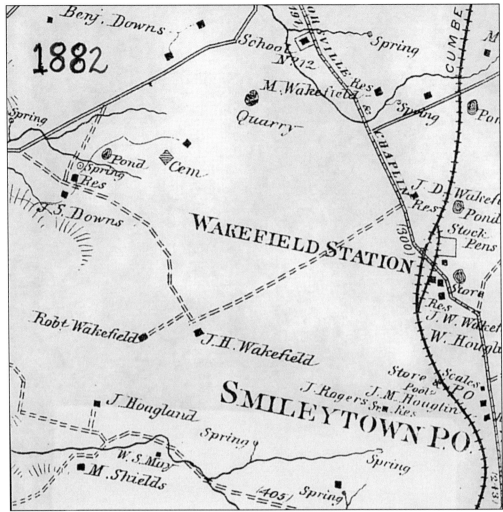

MAY 10, 1865. William C. Quantrill and 20 of his riders stopped at the farm of John Heady Wakefield just across the Nelson-Spencer County line. When it began to rain, they took shelter in the barn and shed. Edwin Terrell, employed by the Federal officials to catch guerrillas about six weeks before and familiar with this guerrilla friendly area, was leading his 30 men on the trail of a cavalry group. He stopped at the blacksmith shop along the Chaplin Pike for information. He was told a group of horsemen had just gone down the road toward the Wakefield farm. They came over the crest of the hill riding hard, and the rain hid them from those in the barn. Suddenly, one of the guerrillas yelled, "Here they come, here they come." One report has Quantrill dozing in the loft of the barn, others had indulged in the horseplay of a corncob fight, indicating they were unaware of any threats. Accounts indicate the guerrillas were taken by complete surprise with unsaddled horses. Quantrill was unable to catch his frightened horse. Hockensmith and Glasscock were mounted and were headed toward an orchard when Glasscock slowed to allow Quantrill to mount behind him. His horse was hit by fire and became unmanageable. Hockensmith came back to help and while trying to mount behind him, Quantrill was shot close to the spine, paralyzing him from the waist down.

MAY 10, 1865. Hockensmith and Glasscock were both killed, and Terrell would claim the shot which mortally wounded Quantrill. Terrell allowed Quantrill to be taken to the Wakefield house where he questioned him while his men continued to chase the fleeing guerrillas. Some of Terrell's men plundered the Wakefield home, until they were paid by the owner to stop. Terrell agreed to leave Quantrill with Wakefield. Dr. McClaskey determined that the wound would be fatal. The news spread that "Captain Clark was mortally wounded at Wakefield's." Visitors during the evening included the judge of Spencer County and Frank James, who was at the Sayers house in Nelson County when he heard of the fight. James offered to rescue him, but Quantrill knew it was useless. He was taken to a military hospital in Louisville in a wagon two days later. He was transferred to a Catholic hospital shortly before he died on June 6th, and was buried in an unmarked grave in Portland Cemetery. Sources differ over the number and names of those with Quantrill at Wakefield. Besides Clark Hockensmith and David Glasscock, who were killed, these men were in Kentucky at the time: Bill Hulse, John Ross, Dave Hilton, Allen Parmer, Lee McMurtry, Isaac and Bob Hall, Payne Jones, John Barnhill, A. D. and Bud Pence, Jackie Graham, John Harris, Ran Venable, Andy McGuire, Jim Lilly (Little), Tucker Basham, Sylvester Akers, Tom Evans, Henry Noland, Henry Porter, and Jim Younger. This is a pre-war photograph of William Clarke Quantrill.

JUNE 1865. John S. Jackman, ex-soldier and lawyer, in an interview in *The Louisville Post* in 1882, told of his acquaintance with the James boys. "I accepted a situation at Samuel's Depot, and as the headquarters of Porter's band was in that vicinity I saw a great deal of them. Frank told me that Jesse had been wounded in Missouri and left behind when Quantrill brought the band to Kentucky. I boarded with Mr. A. Sayers, a short distance from the Depot, and Frank stopped there a great portion of his time, while the negotiations with General Palmer were pending. One night we heard horsemen ride up to Mr. Sayers' gate and give two or three 'Hellos.' Frank James and I were sleeping in a room upstairs and heard the summons and Mr. Sayers' response. When Sayers went out and talked with them, Frank recognized the voice of the speaker as One-Armed-Berry."

JUNE 1865. "Mrs. Sayers came upstairs with a shotgun and told Frank that Berry was after him with 40 men and was going to take him dead or alive. Frank had a pair of Navy pistols, and after dressing himself he moved his bed closer to the door and laid the pistols and shotgun on it and stood ready to sweep the stairway if anyone started up. He then made me crawl out on the portico and listen to the conversation between Berry and Mr. Sayers, and I heard Berry say he had 40 men back out on the road and he knew that Frank James was in the house, and if the latter did not surrender they would surround the house and take him dead or alive. Mr. Sayres assured Berry and his companion that Frank was not in the house, but they insisted that he was. I told Frank what they were saying, and he replied that if the two of them would start upstairs after him he would make it very interesting for them; but they finally rode off.". Above is a photograph of Frank James, taken during the 1890s.

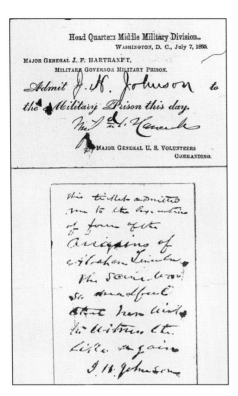

JULY 7, 1865. This pass to the Military Prison, the Old Penitentiary in Washington D.C., was given to J. H. Johnson on July 7, 1865. It was found in Nelson County, Kentucky, but without any information about Mr. Johnson. On the reverse is written "This ticket admitted me to the execution of four of the assassins of Abraham Lincoln, the scene was so dreadful that none wish to witness the like again. J. H. Johnson, July 7, 1865." The four, George Atzerodt, David Herold, Lewis Paine, and Mrs. Mary Surratt, were tried and convicted June 30th, of being conspirators in the assassination.

JULY 26, 1865. Fifteen of the Remainder of Quantrill's group surrendered under Capt. Henry Porter to Captain Young, US Army at Samuel's Depot, Nelson County, and were paroled. According to a comparison of various accounts, the Quantrill riders who were surrendered by Captain Porter to Captain Young, U.S. Army at Samuel's Depot, were Isaac Hall, Bob Hall, John Harris, David Helton, William Hulse, Frank James, Payne Jones, James Lilly, Andy McGuire, Lee McMurtry, Allen H. Parmer, Bud Pence, Donnie Pence, John Ross, Randall Venable, and Jim Younger.

SEPTEMBER 18, 1865. Seven soldiers were arrested for the theft of three barrels of whiskey from railroad cars. Other soldiers testified they awoke to find the camp kettles filled with whiskey. Four of them were indicted and released on bond to Colonel Adams. They did not return in April 1866 for their trial. Whiskey was shipped by James Coy, a local merchant.

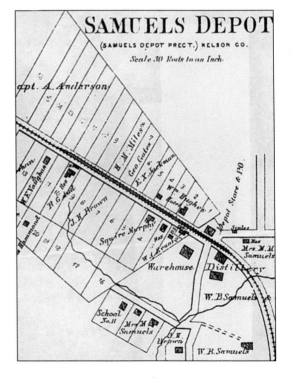

Spring 1868. John Jackman's interview with The *Louisville Post* included this story. "The first I met Jesse James was in the Spring of 1868, he was recuperating from his lung wound. About that time the Russellville bank robbery had occurred. George Sheppard and the Youngers were living in the Chaplin area and Jesse expressed interest in visiting with them. I told him that others didn't hold them as high. The Russellville bank robbery had been talked of by everybody until one day, as the train passed, the conductor told me that Yankee Bligh and Jack Gallagher had gone to Chaplin and arrested Sheppard on suspicion of being connected with the Russellville affair. As soon as I could find Jesse James I took him out to one side and told him what I had heard, and advised him not to associate with any of that gang. Said I: Jesse, you are young and inexperienced; you are a stranger here comparatively, and if you were seen in company with any of these characters, you might be arrested too, and I don't think you would live very long in jail in your present condition. He thanked me kindly for my advice, and expressed great sorrow at what he had considered his old friend Sheppard's misfortune." Jesse James is pictured here.

SPRING 1868. Jackman continues "Mrs. Sheppard, distressed that she couldn't get anybody to go bail for her husband, began to spill her beans. She said that while Jesse was visiting her uncle near Russellsville, he had sent word to Sheppard, that the bank belonged to the meanest old Union man in the County, and that they ought to take some of his money away from him. He had told the Youngers and Sheppard to meet Frank at Russellville to rob the bank. Jackman says that the more Mrs. Sheppard began to talk, the quicker Jesse's wound seemed to heal. Pretty soon he disappeared from Samuel's Depot." The Dawson family history includes Martha Sanders Shepherd telling that she sewed gold pieces from the Russellville Bank Robbery on her coats. She covered them with black cloth and used them like buttons until there was no longer any danger of being apprehended by "the law."

NOVEMBER 1864. This gold framed deguerrotype is of Martha Sanders Maddox. At the time, she was riding with her husband Dick Maddox in Confederate uniform under the name Matt Sanders. It was claimed that she acted as a spy for the Confederate troops. This image shows her with pistol in hand. J. P. Burch, who rode with Quantrill, noted in November 1864, during a battle with a Federal Cherokee group, that she would not stay under cover but "commenced to shoot at the enemy and had a lock of her hair shot off just above the ear." She married George Shepherd after Dick Maddox was killed, right after the war. Shepherd was sent to prison, and she thought that allowed her an immediate divorce. She then married Alex McMakin in Chaplin. When Shepherd was released from prison, she obtained a divorce, and some say he was paid money not to make a fuss. Then she remarried Mr. McMakin. Family stories tell of the fine horses she always rode, sidesaddle of course. Some members of the family considered her conduct "outrageous."

Summer 1881. The two-story, light-colored building on the right is the Central Hotel. In this lobby in 1881, Jesse and Frank James narrowly missed being arrested by detectives Yankee Bligh and George Hunter. The detectives brought two others for reinforcement as they went into the hotel, but Donnie Pence and Ben Johnson joined the James brothers. Jesse walked through the lobby with his arms crossed over his chest and his hands under his coat. He turned and stood while the others walked out the door. After they brought the horses from the nearby livery stable, they quickly mounted and left. Knowing a gunfight would be deadly, the detectives backed off and the James boys rode away. The livery stable is the building on the left with the large posters on the side.

OCTOBER 18, 1881. Jesse James was visiting at Donnie Pence's home (pictured) at Samuel's Depot, Kentucky. Ben Johnson, later Congressman from Kentucky, was introduced to Jesse by Pence when they were out hunting. At the dinner table with others who knew Jesse under his alias, "Thomas Howard," they were interrupted by someone, maybe Belle Pence, who walked in with a newspaper and said, "Look here, the James boys robbed a train yesterday in Missouri." This infuriated Jesse and he took the floor, announced that it was impossible because he was in Samuel's Depot, Kentucky, that day. He stepped to the window where he took his diamond ring and engraved October 18, 1881, and his name, to prove he could not have committed the robbery.

OCTOBER 18, 1881. This may have been the last visit of James to Kentucky before he was killed in 1882 by Bob Ford in St. Joseph, Missouri. How many other places Jesse James did this pane autographing is not known, but scratching names on the glass panes was quite common at the time. In 1931, A. W. Sherman, who owned the Pence house, had the pane of glass removed before the house was torn down. It was preserved by Sherman's grandson, Lowell Ashe, who left it to the Kentucky Historical Society at his death. Pictured is a museum display of Jesse's hat, Donnie Pence's picture, and, to the upper right, a framed photo of the window pane.

A post-war story entitled "Courageous Kentucky Lady" is told by an ex-Confederate soldier: "Bragg was preparing to move from Bardstown. Gen. Wheeler ordered the 1st Ky. to get some wagons from the country to move our sick or otherwise disabled as where then in town. I was detailed to take about 15 men, go on a hunt for the neccssary vehicles. Three miles west and a little south of west of Bardstown, we saw 4 or 5 negroes coming across a field with horses and plows. Riding up to the house towards which they were going. I told an elderly lady who appeared that I had orders to get some wagons in which to move our side and added when her hands got to the road I would have them put the horses to two wagons which were standing near. 'You won't do any such a thing!' She said, coming straight at me. 'Oh I guess I will.' I replied. 'Which side do you belong to Madam?' 'That's none of your business! I have been imposed on by both sides long enough. I'll take no more of it!' Each man of us had a saber, a pistol and a double barreled shotgun; but I was completely whipped. As the enemy was known to be pressing toward town, we hurried back. When we got there the Texas boys were being driven in from the fairgrounds. If we had gotten the wagons, the Yankees would have gotten us." Pictured here is Kentucky currency used during the war.

OCTOBER 22, 1881. In the congregational part of the cemetery at Gethsemane Abbey is the grave of the sister of the Confederate President Jefferson Davis. Her children erected a tall granite monument on which is etched: "To the Memory of our Beloved Mother, Amanda Davis born November 14, 1800; married in Louisiana to David Bradford. Baptised in the Holy Catholic Faith at Nazareth, Ky., taking the baptismal name, Amanda Jane Frances Bradford. Died at New Hope, Ky., in her eighty-first year, October 22, 1881. May She Rest in Peace." Her four daughters attended Nazareth College in the 1840s and converted to Catholicism. They also converted their mother. She was baptized on April 7, 1849. By her daughter's marriage, she became related to the Miles family of Nelson County who were benefactors of the Abbey.

SUMMER 1865. An article in *The Southern Bivouac* read "After the close of the war the graves of sixty-five dead comrades were found by some returning Confederates in an open commons near Bardstown. T. H. Ellis, with one or two others, managed to raise thirteen dollars from the neighbors. With this they bought plank, and having borrowed the tools necessary, they went to work and restored the mounds and fenced them in. Through an old citizen who had taken the pains to keep a register of the places and names of the dead, they erected headboards and set out some young trees. The saplings are now shade trees and the place is kept clean and beautiful by Mrs. P. M. Kelley."

OCTOBER 11, 1905. The Confederate Monument is erected in the Bardstown Cemetery by the Memorial Association of Bardstown, of which Mrs. A. B. Baldwin is President. "The monument is erected to the memory of the sixty seven brave men, buried here . . . ." Mrs. Baldwin's untiring efforts have been crowned with success. The cost of the monument was $900, and though the funds raised fell short, she and her husband donated the balance. She hands the monument over to the Crepps Wickliffe Chapter, U.D.C. of Bardstown.

Bibliography

Allison, Young E. *The Old Kentucky Home*. Bardstown: My Old Kentucky Home Commission Federal Hill, 1923.

An Atlas of Nelson and Spencer Counties, Kentucky. Philadelphia: D.S. Lake and Co., 1882.

Barton, O.S. *Three Years With Quantrell, A True Story*. New York: BuffaloHead Press, 1966.

Blackburn, J.K.P. *Terry's Texas Rangers, Reminiscences of J.K.P. Blackburn*. Austin: 1979.

Bowman, John S. *Who was who in the Civil War*. Greenwich, Connecticut: Brompton Books Corp. and Sweetwater Press, 1998.

Burch, J.P. *A True Story of Chas W. Quantrel*. Texas: J.P. Burch Vega, 1923.

Bush, Bryan S. *The Civil War Battles of the Western Theatre*. Paducah, Kentucky: Turner Publishing Company, 1998.

Collins, Lewis. *History of Kentucky*. Covington, Kentucky: Collins and Company, 1874.

Confederate Veteran Magazine. Collector Historical Prints Inc., July-Aug. 1993.

Davis, William C. *Diary of a Confederate Soldier*. Columbia, South Carolina: University of South Carolina Press, 1990.

Davis, William C. and Bell I. Wiley. *The Civil War*. New York: Workman Publishing Company, 1998.

Duke, Basil W. *Morgan's Cavalry*. New York, Washington 1906.

Elliot, Sam Carpenter. *The Nelson County Record*. Bardstown, Kentucky: The Record Printing Co., 1896.

Hafendorfer, Kenneth A. *They Died by Twos and Tens*. Louisville: K.H. Press, 1995.

History of Bloomfield Baptist Church, Two Hundredth Anniversary.

Johnston, Col. J. Stoddard and Col. John C. Moore. *Kentucky and Missouri, Confederate Military History*. The Blue and Grey Press. Vol. IX.

McDogough, James Lee. *War in Kentucky from Shiloh to Perryville*. University of TN. Press, 1994.

Military History of Kentucky. Frankfort, Kentucky: Works Progress Administration, 1930.

Reid. *Ohio in the War*. Vol. II. Kentucky Historical Society.

Report of Adjutant General. Union Soldiers and Sailors Monument Association KHR.

Report of the Adjutant General of the State of Kentucky. *Confederate, Kentucky Volunteers, Civil War 1861-65*. Utica, Kentucky: Printed by Authority of the Legislature of Kentucky, McDowell Publications, 1980.

Roll of Honor, Names of Soldiers who Died in Defense of the American Union. U.S. Quartermasters Dept.

Scribner, B.F. *How Soldiers were made or The War as I saw it*. New Albany, Ind. 1887.

Smith, Sarah B. *Historic Nelson County, Its Town and People*. Bardstown, Kentucky: GBA/Delmar, 1983.

Speed, Thomas, R.M. Kelly and Alfred Pirtle. *The Union Regiments of Kentucky*. Louisville 1897.

Swiggett, Howard. *The Rebel Raider*. Indianapolis: The Bobbs Merril Company, 1934.

Tarrant, Sergeant E. *The Wild Riders of the First Kentucky Cavalry*. A Committee of the Regiment.

The Filson Club History Quarterly, Louisville: July 1970, Jan. 1975, April 1984, April 1972, Oct. 1987, April 1978, April 1967, Jan. 1964, Jan. 1973.

The Register of the Kentucky Historical Society. Frankfort: Oct. 1973, Jan. 1977.

Thomas, John B. Jr. *A History of Nelson County Newspapers*. Kentucky Standard in 198485.

Thomas, John B. Jr. *A History of the Civil War in Nelson County, Kentucky*

Watson, Thomas Shelby "Bob." *The Silent Riders*. Louisville: Beechmont Press, 1971.

Workers of the Federal Writers Project of the Works Progress Administration for the state of Kentucky. *War of the Rebellion, Official Records of the Union and Confederate Armies*. Washington: Government Printing Office, 1890.

Acknowledgments

A series of newspaper articles in *The Kentucky Standard* in 198788, by John B. Thomas, stimulated my interest in the Civil War history of Nelson County. He is a native of Bloomfield, Kentucky, who now lives in Silver Springs, Maryland. As I researched references to the war in the county I realized I was following in his footsteps through the extensive records. I sometimes added information, but always relied on his detailed stories. With his kind permission, a substantial part of this book is based on his articles

    Thank you to the following Civil War enthusiasts: Richard Stone, who supplied me with materials, drove me around country roads to take photographs, and reacted to the information I was uncovering; Larry Frye, of Maryland, who supplied me with the 7th PA Cav. information; Charles Lemons, who has researched the war in New Haven and kindly let me use his material; Jude Wheatley, who shared the Samuel Calhoun book with me; Henry Sutherland, who had the picture of the Sutherland homeplace; and Sam Cecil who shared his books and gun with me. Others who wished to remain unnamed also shared materials with me.

    I used the research facilities of the Filson Club Historical Society, the group that allowed me to quote from the Alfred Pirtle Journal of 1861; the Louisville Public Library (microfilm newspaper collection); the Bardstown Civil War Museum; the Nelson County Public Library; the Kentucky Historical Society Library and Special Collections.

Personal thanks go to Mary Winter of the KHS Special Collections for her help; Becky Dunn, for help in reading microfilm, typing lists, and other dull work; Laura Gilkerson, for proofing with patience and understanding; and last but most thanks go to Janice Donan, whose gift of time, computer expertise, and personal friendship allows me to take history out of my head and put it on to paper.

    My husband, Franklin, proofread and critiqued the content, sometimes to my dismay, but always in a constructive way. His vital support was appreciated.

Photo Credits

The letter *a* indicates the top picture on the page, *b* the lower one. Any pictures not listed below belong to the author's collection.

Bloomfield Baptist Church: 53; Emily Dawson: 80, 96, 11, 120, 121; Larry Frye: 107; Stephen G.Hayden: 23a; *Harpers Weekly* Magazine: 16b, 17, 32b, 37b, 78a, 93; Carl Howell: 37a; Jailer's Inn: 30; Kentucky Historical Society Special Collections: 2, 10, 12, 14, 20, 21, 28, 31, 33, 38, 44, 51, 52b, 85, 102, 115, 119; Charles Lemons: 8b; *Frank Leslie Newspaper*: 15b, 35, 35a, 36b, 42a 50. 69, 76; Library of Congress: 27, 39a, 34b, 48b, 54b, 60a, 68, 112b; *Louisville Journal*: 20; Military Order of the Loyal Legion and the U.S. Army Military History Institute: 5, 34a, 39b, 58, 61, 62; W. F. Monfort Collection: 13, 105, 117; John W. Muir Collection: 27a, 45, 55, 63b, 84a,101b,116, 122,123; Sisters of Charity of Nazareth Archives: 47, 63a, 67b, 73, 108; Smith Collection:118; Henry Sutherland: 29; The *Nelson County Record of* 1896:100; Mrs. Sara Trigg: 97, 106; Guthrie M. Wilson: 40; Mary Annette Wimpsett: 106.